*The Complete Guide to
Gay and Lesbian Weddings*

The Complete Guide to

GAY *and* LESBIAN WEDDINGS

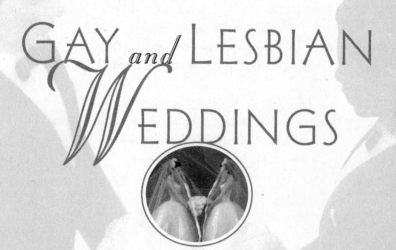

K. C. David

and the Experts at GayWeddings.com

Photography by Wendy Paton

THOMAS DUNNE BOOKS ✠ ST. MARTIN'S GRIFFIN
NEW YORK

THOMAS DUNNE BOOKS.
An imprint of St. Martin's Press.

www.stmartins.com

Book design by Richard Oriolo

Library of Congress Cataloging-in-Publication Data
David, Keith C.
 The complete guide to gay and lesbian weddings / Keith C.
David, and the experts at GayWeddings.com
  p. cm.
 ISBN 0-312-33879-1
 EAN 978-0-312-33879-4
 1. Same-sex marriage, 2. Weddings—Handbooks, manuals,
 etc. I. Title.

HQ1033.D38 2005
395.2'2'08664—dc22   2004063281

FIRST EDITION: June 2005

10 9 8 7 6 5 4 3 2 1

This Book Is Dedicated to Doris

—◦—◦—

When her small-town "religious" friends found out she was a lesbian,
they scorned and abandoned her. Her family disowned her.
She thought she was alone with nowhere to turn . . . all
simply because she was trying to come out of the
darkness and be who she really was.

And when it seemed that there was no more hope, only more
darkness, she took her life out of desperation.

We hope that she is somehow able to feel all of the incredible
love these wedding couples have for each other. She, above
all, would understand that they're just celebrating the
infinite diversity of God's creation and
His unconditional love.

Because of Doris, and the trials she endured, there's now
more hope in this world. It's a hope that was born and then
blossomed because of her pain; her gift to all of us.

Contents

Introduction

"You have to love your partner for who they really are.

I don't want to make her into just some mirror image

of who I am. That wouldn't be fair."

HEATHER

Love Is Love in All Its Forms

When St. Martin's Press approached me and my dedicated team to do a book about gay weddings, and all of the many details that are associated with the subject, I felt confident that my exceptional team and I could handle the challenge. I am now openly gay and have been in a long-term relationship with my partner. In fact, in 2002, after being together for over eleven years, we had a wonderful ceremony of our own in the captivating state of Vermont at Castle Hill, an incredible property constructed at the turn of the century. Our ceremony took place in their Old World library, which was an outstanding setting.

I personally have over ten years of experience as a wedding consultant at the 8-Diamond inn and restaurant that Doc and I own and operate together in Bucks County, Pennsylvania. Then of course there's the website, GayWeddings.com, which I launched in 1998, where we have helped hundreds of couples plan their ceremonies and find everything from attorneys to resources for starting a family.

If anybody was qualified to write a book covering gay weddings, I thought I might be, along with my excellent staff. I certainly have had a great deal of experience with gay weddings, but underneath this bravado, there was a part of me that was still apprehensive about the whole thing. There seemed to me to be a nagging question that still was lingering in the back of my head after all this time: How would I make this book different from other "traditional" wedding books that were already out there?

With the encouragement of my team at GayWeddings.com, I decided to take on the challenge, and together we resolved to write a wedding book that would be a unique guide to planning your wedding day, geared solely toward the gay and lesbian community.

The decision was made, the contract was signed and . . . I was outta there! I decided we should start our "research" right away, so we split to attend a gay wedding of friends of ours in Capri, Italy! You understand that I considered this trip to be about nothing but business and research, right? Right!

Doc and I spent three fantastic days and nights on the beautiful island of Capri, celebrating the wedding of these two very special friends. In between the festivities, of course, we had to swim, sun ourselves, and visit the Blue Grotto.

During all of the festivities, I would think about the book (from time to time) and ask myself how this couple's ceremony was different from any other traditional couple's wedding. There really didn't seem to be much difference at all, other than the fact that they were both the same sex. I couldn't come up with a ready answer. I couldn't think about it for long because with everything going on, I found myself distracted again. There would be another toast to the couple and I'd be back in party mode once again! "Book? What book?"

After the wedding, we were off to the exquisite coast city of Positano for another two weeks' extended "work leave." Now I could really focus on the tasks at hand—relaxing and eating wonderful food! "No, no, the book," I reminded myself. "I'm supposed to be figuring out how these weddings are different from all of the other straight wedding guides, remember?"

There were the blatantly obvious differences that everyone recognizes between gay weddings and traditional ones: two brides, two grooms. I've learned over the years that gay and lesbian weddings are also usually much more creative than straight weddings in their style and presentation. And there was no doubt in my mind that every one that I had attended was truly moving and tugged at the heartstrings. (And I will admit that my feelings were influenced by my sexual orientation and life experience, no doubt about that.) It does take a lot of courage not only to stand up at that altar, but also to stand up and be who you truly are. That's for sure.

There seemed to be another difference, too. Gay couples didn't seem to feel the need to follow a traditionally outlined format, down to the letter, like most straight couples do. At the gay weddings I attended, the couples were never afraid to follow their hearts and show deep emotion when it bubbled up from within them.

At dinner the last night of our stay in Positano, Doc and I sat staring out over the harbor lights and the sea. Off in the distance we heard a mandolin playing "Santa Lucia." As I sat there slowly sipping my wine and taking it all in, I remembered the laughter and tears we had been part of at our friends' wedding just a few days before. These were very familiar feelings to me. They were the same warm feelings of love and hope that had been expressed at our wedding and at all weddings, straight or gay, that I'd ever attended.

And then I realized how my wedding book could be different from all the other wedding books out there: It could clarify that, in reality, there aren't any major differences between gay and straight weddings. Love is love in all its many forms!

The book produced by GayWeddings.com would be written for gay and lesbian couples who were planning a wedding, but we would also be inclusive. Traditional straight couples could also read it if they wanted to, to gather ideas from our community. Our book would be different in that its target audience would be gays and straights together, but always with an emphasis on the same-sex couples that we were trying to help. Ours would be an all-inclusive guide, addressing the issues and concerns of prenuptial couples and the attending straight guests.

It's fitting that the concept for this book should have been born in Italy, the land of romance and love. (Did I mention that Doc is Italian, from Milan?) That's a big part of what weddings should be about: romance and love. Don't you think? Add to that a mixture of compassion, sincerity, courage, commitment, and the need to express who we really are, and you'll be close to knowing what it is to be one of the people having a gay wedding.

This book is intended to help couples decide what it is they want for their special day. It will also give their family, friends, and guests an understanding of why gay marriage is so important. It is intended to help our couples not only in the planning of their ceremony (and all the many details associated with it), but also in expressing what it is they truly want on their wedding day. We want to help them make their dreams a reality.

Please keep in mind that almost everyone who attends the ceremony of a same-sex couple will be changed in one way or another. Why? Because they will see that no matter what outside form this special occasion takes, inside . . . love is love in all its forms.

No matter what anyone says, we all do have the right to believe in the dream that we can have a life partner, a marriage, and even kids if we choose to have them. So with all of that said . . . let's plan a wedding! Let's make it a day that you and your partner will never forget! We're here to help guide you to that goal as best we can.

Remember that the key to discovering what it is you and your partner want for your wedding lies in your expression of who you are as a couple. Bottom line: If you let your love shine through on your wedding day, you will have made the perfect wedding, no matter what.

Both of you, in our own way, are doing your part to help to change the way this country thinks and feels about the gay community. Go ahead and ask anyone who's attended one of these celebrations. They are always deeply touched and moved by the experience. When the two of you stand up at that altar, or by that lake, or on that mountaintop, proclaiming the love you have for each other, the people standing near you are going to say, "Wow! That was incredible!"

Trust us, we know what we're talking about. All of your fears, anxieties, and apprehensions will be blown away in that brief moment and the hours that follow. And you both will know, for certain, that you are meant to be living a shared dream together and that the dream is possible. It's the same dream that all straight couples have had for centuries, and finally now, our community is rightfully sharing that dream too, right alongside them.

Oh, and by the way, from all of us at GayWeddings.com . . . Congratulations! May you both be an example to the entire world of what love can truly be.

K. C. DAVID
President, GayWeddings.com

What Is Gay Weddings.com?

In 1998, Hawaii was considering whether or not to let same-sex couples have the right to marry. We saw an opportunity to launch a community website that would cover every aspect of the development of the same-sex marriage issue. We wanted it to be an online resource center for couples who wanted to find ways to legally protect themselves and their assets. We also wanted it to be a place where our couples could plan weddings and feel at home, finding gay-friendly businesses and people who didn't have a negative attitude toward the gay community.

After a frustrating first year, our team was growing discouraged just trying to find gay-friendly places for our couples to have their ceremonies. We've made significant progress over the years, I'm proud to say. We began to discover that there were a lot of supportive people and companies out there who, once they learned what this issue of human rights and equality was all about, wanted to help our community and be part of the team. These businesses took a stand for us when we needed it most. They were, and continue to be, good people who have a sense of fairness and know the importance of equality for everyone.

One of the first good people who listed with us and offered his encouragement and help was Ken Richardson, who owns the Black Bear Inn in Vermont. During the "Take Back Vermont" campaign, it took guts for him to stand up for his beliefs on equal rights. My, how things have changed over the past six years! Now, well over three hundred Fortune 500 companies are offering some kind of partnership plans (up from just over thirty companies when GayWeddings.com was launched). Multi-national corporate advertising has made its way into the top gay publications. Corporate America has discovered the untapped market of the gay and lesbian community, which has large disposable incomes and assets estimated in 2004 by Forbes at well over 513 billion dollars!

As gay culture becomes more accepted by the mainstream, our website has begun to grow profoundly. Now, some of the top hotels and inns across the country are getting on board. We're even beginning to book wedding packages internationally.

We have people coming from all over the world to have their ceremonies here in the U.S. Part of the reason for this is their belief that America still represents the land of freedom and hope. It's our belief in the right to freedom and equal rights, as well as our ceaseless hope, that keeps all of us at GayWeddings.com working hard to help our community however we can, in whatever ways we can.

The two of you as a couple, standing up for who you are and the love you share, continue to help change our country for the better. We believe this from the bottom of our hearts. You are showing our country what love for another person (no matter how different it may seem to some) truly is. Thank you to all of you from our community who have let us share in your love and commitment along the way. You continue to give us hope and encouragement for our community and what it stands for.

THE TEAM AT GAYWEDDINGS.COM

Why the Right to Marry?

Considering the severity of the many serious problems facing our nation—national security, global unrest, poverty here and abroad, the destruction of the planet, the volatile economy—I can't help but ask myself, "Why is this idea of same-sex marriage such a hotly debated topic right now?"

It's easy for us to understand why we in the gay community have just as much right to marriage as the straight community. Marriage, and everything it symbolizes, helps to lead all of us in the gay community to equality. Marriage is a legal status that comes with rights and responsibilities, and these rights include recognition for our family structures. I believe, and many others do too, that the gay and lesbian community should be entitled to exactly the same legal rights that the heterosexual community in America now automatically enjoys.

If we as consenting adults in this country do not have the more than one thousand federal rights that traditional marriage grants, we will always be considered second-class citizens, no matter how you look at it. Legalizing same-sex marriages validates these unions and affirms the commitment between two loving individuals. This validation allows others to see two individuals as one unit, a couple: two yet one, sharing their love.

In the past, there weren't very many public acknowledgments of long-term gay relationships. Part of the reason for this was that many of these relationships were very discreet, and these couples chose to stay out of the public eye for many reasons, including fear of rejection from family, employers, and the straight community in general. Prejudice and ignorance about gay people helped the media to paint a picture of a promiscuous portion of society—when it revealed any information about the gay community at all—omitting any evidence of stability, commitment, or long-term partnerships.

When all is said and done, equality in marriage is vital to the future of our community. Many people do not understand that, at present, same-sex couples . . .

+ . . . are being denied the right to see their partner in a hospital if the partner is unconscious or in critical condition.

+ . . . cannot move into a nursing home with their partner because of a lack of marriage rights.

+ . . . who have lived with and loved their partner for decades have lost entire estates—sometimes everything they owned—because assets could not legally be left to their partner since they were not joined in marriage.

+ . . . do not have access to the over one thousand federal rights of protection granted through marriage.

Where is the "liberty and justice for all" we have been brought up to believe in? Thank God things continue to change!

One small but very important example of this change is the *New York Times,* which now regularly showcases gay and lesbian couples as a matter of policy in their wedding section. As more gay community members stand up for themselves and their relationships, more and more Americans are beginning to slowly take a new look at this long-ignored and concealed segment of society. Contrary to popular belief and prejudice, it is a portion of the population that does care about commitment, "family values," and love for children. Not very different from most conservative thinkers, huh? It makes you wonder why more politicians still don't support our choice to marry!

Some in the gay community argue that by marriage we are just mimicking straight society, when in reality, we just want to be recognized and validated for loving another person, a partner with whom we want to share our life. A civil or religious ceremony and exchange of rings gives us that public validation. The more weddings we've seen among our gay and lesbian friends, the more we realize that gay people are not trying to imitate straight society by marrying, we are simply forming bonds and trying to acquire the same civil rights.

Why should we have the right to marry? Because we are consenting, tax-paying adults and we should not be discriminated against just because we are in love with someone of the same sex. If it disturbs conservative states because we call it "marriage," we say get over it, find another name for it if you absolutely have to, but just give us the same one thousand plus rights straight couples gain through marriage. You can call it what you want, but we will still call it marriage!

Of course, sadly, with the world being what it is, we have to be aware of the prejudices and homophobia that unfortunately still exist. There are many arguments against same-sex marriages. Most of them are ridiculous, to say the least. After all, this is America, the land of the free, indivisible, with liberty and justice for all. It's the land led by We The People, right? Well, aren't *we* part of the people?

For now we may have to call it a "civil union," instead of "marriage," but it is a commitment that should not be denied to any consenting adult couple that wants that choice. We are not talking religion here, we are talking civil rights! We as a community are simply asking for equality under the law. It's as simple as that. And this issue will not go away . . . not until every state in our wonderful union realizes that it is a matter of equality and civil rights, no matter how you decide to spell it!

Let Me Give It to You Straight

As children we were told that when you grew up you'd fall in love, get married, and have a family. Most of our parents didn't offer us options or even consider that we might be attracted to the same sex. Well, guess what Mom and Dad? As it turns out, that traditional equation just doesn't necessarily hold true for everybody!

Not so long ago, if you happened to be gay or lesbian, you were not expected to want to marry someone of the same sex. And yet, there were very many gays and lesbians in committed relationships who still wanted to marry, no matter what anyone said.

In 1998, when I started GayWeddings.com, sexual preference was being explored openly, and "commitment ceremony" was becoming an increasingly popular term for a gay "wedding." Gay couples had been having these ceremonies for years and finally the subject of gay committed relationships was getting its long-overdue time in the spotlight. Favorite gay characters like Will and Jack (from *Will & Grace*) were becoming icons in the cultural mainstream. News organizations were beginning to cover gay-related topics more often, and the American audience was becoming more comfortable with the subject in general. Gay people from all over were making strides in attaining equality and erasing stigmas and stereotypes, each in their own way.

But the issue of gay marriage lingered as a specter of inequity. Gay people can pay taxes, entertain the masses, bear children, and become CEOs or politicians. In some, but not all, states, they may adopt children. Some religions allow gay clergy members . . . but they are still not able to marry in all of the United States except Massachusetts.

The thousands of couples who sought information from

GayWeddings.com when Vermont offered civil unions should affirm to anyone that love and commitment have nothing to do with sexual orientation. I talked with hundreds of these couples when the website was launched. They called and said that they wanted to go to Vermont to legitimize their relationships. They were the pioneers who didn't care what it meant back in their home states. These couples were simply asking, "Why shouldn't we be allowed to marry when we're in love, just like any other couple?"

Straight people are beginning to realize that their brothers, sisters, sons, daughters, and friends should be considered equal citizens with equal rights *at all times*. One day it will be the norm for parents to know that if they have a gay son or daughter, they will be able to find someone, settle down, get married, and live a happy life in a committed relationship. Isn't that what parents really wish for all of their children?

Commitment is about choice. Love and commitment between two adults should be approved of and honored by all facets of our society: church, state, and culture. This will not happen overnight, but the movement is growing stronger every day. It will take the continued and combined effort of the gay and straight communities together to demand rights of marriage for all. And that's what America's supposed to be all about: equality and freedom for all.

CERTIFICATION OF VITAL RECORD

STATE OF VERMONT

DEPARTMENT OF HEALTH
VERMONT LICENSE AND CERTIFICATE
OF CIVIL UNION

1b. MAIDEN SURNAME (If Applicable)

and Number or Rural Route Number, City or Town, State, Zip Code)

TT PLACE, FALLS CHURCH

1c. City or Town

FALLS CHURCH

Legal Planning

and the Ever-Changing Legality of Gay Marriage

"I found out that love doesn't ever die. I know that's hard to believe, but it doesn't. It won't die as long as I let it reside where it rightfully belongs . . . inside the heart."

NANCY, AFTER HER PARTNER'S EARLY DEATH

Most of us have the need for a long-term, committed relationship filled with sharing and love. In our society this type of relationship is called marriage. Historically, the institution of marriage and its laws have continually changed and evolved in the direction of greater inclusion and equality. In the past, most marriages were pre-arranged and the marriage vows reflected the idea that the wife was the husband's property. In the early 1800s, married women gave up their legal rights and were subsumed under the legal identity of their husbands. Only after the Civil War were African Americans allowed to marry in all of the United States.

The civil rights and women's liberation movements have made great strides toward equality by enlightening the world (most of the world, anyway) to the fact that all human beings deserve equal rights. The gay community is indebted to all minorities who struggled to gain and expand equal rights. It is this foundation of activism that encourages our community to work for the right for same-sex marriage.

The birth control pill blew away the idea that marriage was linked to procreation. In 1965 it became legal for married couples to buy and use contraception. (Did everyone really think married straight people were really just having sex just to have babies? Where's the fun in that?) Through the years, it became acceptable for married couples to choose not to have children. Remember that it was only in the '80s when the acronym DINKs (Double Income No Kids) was coined. And as late as 1967, sixteen states outlawed marriage between people of different races.

All of these changes were met with fierce opposition, but eventually our society recognized the inequities of such laws. We tend to forget that these commonly accepted norms were hotly debated issues at one time. We've come a long way, baby, but for same-sex couples these inequities still remain, and we believe that is unfair. Extending marriage to same-sex couples is the obvious next step.

———

Why Marriage?

Marriage is a fundamental desire of many loving same-sex couples who want to share their lives in long-term, committed relationships. They, too, want to have and to hold, in sickness and in health, for better or worse, for richer or poorer, until death do them part. Many same-sex couples are buying homes, raising children, joining churches, and contributing to life in their communities.

Same-sex couples simply want the right to be different, the right to be equal, and the right to receive all of the advantages that opposite-gender couples automatically acquire when they marry. Their needs and concerns are the same as for any married couple:

+ Access to spousal benefits such as Social Security, health insurance, and pensions

+ Access to family/medical and bereavement leave

+ Hospital visitation and medical decision-making for a gravely ill or incapacitated spouse

+ Child custody and visitation rights

+ Significant tax benefits, particularly with regard to owning a home together

+ Automatic right of inheritance

. . . and many, many other federal rights.

Civil marriage offers hundreds of legal protections and obligations, most of which cannot be obtained any other way. These laws provide the guidelines to maneuver through complicated legal and financial situations and deal with serious illness, death, or divorce.

Why marriage? Marriage is universally accepted as a public statement of love. Marriage brings legal benefits. Marriage protects and provides for children. The commitment of marriage helps to maintain the couple's union.

Civil unions provide only a third of the protections of marriage because they do not include many of the significant federal benefits, such as access to a spouse's Social Security. Civil unions are, so far, not yet recognized from state to state.

When Vermont passed the first civil union recognition laws, it was that legislature's attempt to provide broad benefits to the same-sex couples in conformance with the Vermont Supreme Court ruling. It was a step in the right direction—but our laws have a long way to go if they are ever to be recognized on a federal level.

Domestic Partnerships

Many states and cities have passed some kind of domestic partnership laws. They have been enacted in California, Connecticut, New Jersey, Hawaii, and the District of Columbia, among others, but the benefits provided by these laws vary. In some cases they offer access to family health insurance, and others confer co-parenting rights. These benefits are limited and are in no way equal to the automatic rights that traditional straight couples in the U.S. automatically have.

Even if civil unions and domestic partnerships provided all the rights and protections of marriage, many in our community would still cry out that it isn't fair to have same-sex couples delegated to a different category which is separate and not totally equal. Civil unions and domestic partnerships provide some tangible but very limited benefits to same-sex couples and their children. However, these options still keep our community separated from the mainstream of married society. Love should not be measured or defined in terms of sexual orientation.

Protecting Your Relationship and Future Together

If you sincerely love and care about your partner, and plan to build a life together, we strongly suggest that you look into the following to protect your rights:

- Consult with a competent attorney who knows about partnership laws
- Have a civil union wedding or a domestic partnership wedding

(with witnesses) so your intentions to one another are made public

+ Draw up a will and power of attorney for each of you with your attorney

+ Make an Emergency Medical Card (shown on page 6) and put it in your wallet

These four things, in combination, at least help to document your intentions for the courts should there ever be a situation where you have to prove that the two of you are in a relationship and consider yourselves more than just friends or roommates.

A ceremony carries symbolic value, in that you are publicly declaring your commitment to each other in front of witnesses. However, without a civil union or domestic partnership and a durable power of attorney with a living will, you have not taken an important step in documenting that the two of you are in a committed and recognized relationship. If you have no documentation whatsoever, unless the family permits you, you will most likely be barred from the hospital if your partner is ever in a coma, be unable to receive information about your partner's medical condition without a family member present, and not be allowed to participate in making any medical decisions on your partner's behalf. Speak with your attorney, since state laws vary, about what you both can do to protect yourselves from this injustice. Without a will, you or your partner could lose everything you've built and acquired together, including your home and any other assets.

These horror stories unfortunately happen all too frequently. We don't meant to scare you, but an hour of your time with a competent attorney can save a lifetime of heartache for both of you!

When it comes to partnership rights, remember that it does not matter how long the two of you have been together as partners. Most states will regard you as total strangers for the purposes of inheritance, medical decisions, and other critical matters. This is why documentation is so critical.

Generally speaking, your will is a written document that controls the disposal of your property (including real estate, money, other assets, and guardianship) in the event of your death. Your power of attorney is a written instrument that legally authorizes another person to act in your behalf. With health care provisions you can authorize another person to make decisions affecting your medical condition. Again, we cannot stress enough the suggestion that you both find an attorney to help protect yourselves, your assets, and any children that you may have together.

In addition to drawing up these safeguards with your attorney, it is also important to always carry an Emergency Medical Card with you in your purse or wallet. It will provide your attending physicians with your preferred family contact. Your Emergency Medical Card should include the following, and you should carry it next to your driver's license *at all times:*

EMERGENCY MEDICAL CARD | **MEDICAL INFORMATION**

NAME: _____

ADDRESS: _____

_____

_____

PHONE: _____

In an emergency, I authorize you to call

NAME: _____

PHONE: _____

MEDICAL CONDITIONS: _____

_____

_____

_____

ALLERGIES OR MEDICATIONS

_____

_____

_____

AUTHORIZING SIGNATURE

_____

Please note that the information provided in this book is not, and should not be construed as, legal advice. The laws concerning gay rights are constantly evolving and changing. What we are strongly recommending is that each person should consult their attorney concerning legal matters.

Do everything you can to protect your partnership. Keep up with the ever-changing laws and developing protections for the two of you, and above all, set up an appointment with that competent attorney who cares about the important issues that you and your partner are both facing.

We highly recommend that you consult the current laws of your state through LAMBDA, a nonprofit gay and lesbian community agency that provides a full range of community services. Their website is www.lambda.org. Find out what your city or state is currently offering in the way of domestic partnerships or civil unions, since the laws in each state are changing now at a steady rate. There will be gains and other setbacks as our community reaches for its dream of equality under federal law. As with any cause, sometimes it may seem like we are losing the battle, but we must always keep in mind that a setback is just one battle. We believe we will win that "war." Why? Because anyone who knows gay or lesbian couples realizes that they deserve all of the same protections and rights as traditional couples. This lack of equality strikes at the very heart of civil rights, no matter how much anyone tries to detract from it by focusing on morality or religion. You may also refer to the Resources chapter for additional community groups.

(Note: Understand that none of the "suggestions" replace your consulting a competent attorney.)

The Engagement

Love, Commitment, and Popping the Question

"Love at first sight can't ever be forgotten, but the love that lasts a lifetime . . . now that's the greatest gift my partner could have ever given me."

EDWARD

Always keep in mind these three key words: *Make it special!*

Unless you fall into really bad habits—like Liz Taylor did at times—you're not going to be doing this "proposal thing" on a regular basis. So make it as memorable as you can. Even if it's not totally possible, try to make your proposal something that legends are made of, if only in its sincerity and the meaning that you draw on to create this special moment.

We've all heard of the candlelit romantic dinner, the ring inside a glass of champagne. Or maybe a moonlit night on the beach with the waves crashing. You turn to your partner and tell them how much they mean to you. They're caught off guard. You touch their cheek gently, and reaffirm how much meaning they've given to your life, how much you wish that it could last forever. You kiss them gently, looking deeply into their eyes. Slowly, you reach into your pocket, and as a sign of humility and love, you bend down to one knee.* Your partner has a look of surprise on their face. They smile broadly, not sure of what's coming next. You pull out the ring, it flashes in the moonlight, and then you say those special words that you've rehearsed over and over. A sonnet written just for them, or words that have special meaning to you both. Words that would bring tears to the eyes of lovers around the world. (No pressure here!) You finish your proposal by saying something like, "I want you in my life. Now and always. I want us to be committed to each other. I want to face the world with you, to spend my life with you. Will you marry me?"

How and where you ask this special question will be unique to you. Many couples go back to the original place where they met, or to a place that has special meaning to both of them. Some take their partner to their favorite restaurant or take a trip together and find a quiet romantic spot to pop the question.

If you're the one doing the asking, three words of advice here . . . *make it special!* There's certainly some thought and planning to do beforehand if you are the one who will be doing the asking. Think about your partner. Ask yourself the question, "What will make this a memorable occasion for both of us?"

Deep down you know what touches your partner's heart. Move them with the sincerity of your love. If you're sincere, that's all it's going to take for them to know that what you say is true. You don't have to necessarily write it on a billboard or in smoky letters across the sky.

---

*Author's Note: My sister, after reading this far, said to me, "Pleeeaase! I'm not doing it that way! Can you please lighten up a bit?" So with her straightforward advice in mind, whatever your style might be, just do what feels right for you, okay?

Just try to make your proposal something that shows you've put your love and heart into it, and that you mean it with all of that heart.

No matter where you make the proposal, no matter how you do it, if you are sincere the proposal will become a lasting memory that lingers for a lifetime in the heart of your partner. And remember through all of this, it doesn't have to be perfect. Nothing ever is. Keep your sense of humor. The combination of love and humor is essential for making memorable moments throughout your life together.

My partner took me to my favorite local restaurant and chose a table off by ourselves. He prearranged it with the owner, telling her it was a special occasion. He knew that she knew us as a couple and that the table would be away from prying ears. He ordered champagne, laid a rose on the table, and said to me, "I know sometimes I don't say it often enough, but my life is so much more because you're in it."

I looked at him and he was smiling from ear to ear. I had no idea what was coming next, I really didn't. I just thought he was paying me a great and heartfelt compliment. I said to him that my life was richer, too, and that he helped to make me feel complete.

He put a ring box on my plate and I looked at him in confusion. The waiter started to come over, not knowing what was going on, and my partner said, "Please, not now, just give us a minute." The waiter nodded and walked away.

I said, "You didn't have to do that," or something to that effect, thinking that he had bought me a new pair of cufflinks for some reason. He told me to open the box. I lifted the lid, and there was this incredible ring with small diamonds around the band. I looked up and he had tears in his eyes. This big lump came up in my throat. You intuitively know what is coming next in a moment like this. "What is this?" I asked myself, already knowing the answer.

He then asked me to marry him. I think I said yes. I'm not sure because I was so choked up . . . and suddenly, before I knew what was happening. I had the ring on my finger and I was hugging him!

I can honestly tell you that it was at that moment that I didn't care about anybody else in the restaurant looking. It was one of those rare moments in life when time stood still and I felt all the love the world had to give. Even as I write this and recall that moment, I still well up with tears. It's amazing how much a moment like that can stay with you forever. We had been together for twelve years and this was almost three years ago, and yet when I think about it, it still affects me deeply.

Doc didn't make the "popping of the question" elaborate or fancy. He did it with sincerity and love and that was all it took. So our advice to you is that if you're trying to come up with a gimmick to ask the question, don't do it until you first think about who your partner is, and try to find a way that simply shows how much they sincerely mean to you. Think about their passions, their deepest interests, what touches them the most with happiness, and what could you do to make this a memory to last a lifetime. Sometimes, simplicity with love is the best combination of all.

So many of us, as we go through life struggling to deal with identity and same-sex attraction, finally give up on the idea of ever experiencing a moment like this. As we discover that we are gay, marriage is one of those dreams that tends to be thrown out the window. The thought of anyone ever proposing to us seems too far-fetched, just like the thought of ever having children.

I am here to tell you, my friends—those days are gone. It all began with Vermont's first steps at affirming complete equality, and those first steps are beginning to change all of our options. Members of our community are committing themselves to their partners, adopting or having children, and finally realizing that just because we are attracted to the same sex, we don't have to give up our dreams.

There are a thousand ways and places to ask the question "Will you marry me?" We've witnessed quite a few of them at our inn, and each one, no matter how simple, conveyed to the other person how much they were loved. We've seen it in the couple's eyes when we sent complimentary champagne to their table and we've seen it in the moments afterwards when they snuggled on the wicker sofas out on the lawn, under the torches, listening to the classical guitar player.

So whether you're going to write it across a billboard on the highway or ask the question over candlelight and champagne, if you're lucky this will be the night you've waited for all your life. And whether you are doing the asking or your partner is, we hope it will come with all the sincerity, honesty, and love that can be mustered!

—◆—

Your Rings and What They Symbolize

If you have lived together for many years, you may already have rings that symbolize your relationship. You may want to consider keeping them as they are, getting them reworked with a new look, or possibly even getting new ones just for this upcoming special occasion. Many couples engrave the wedding date inside their rings, adding a few words that have great meaning for both of the partners. This is a new beginning for both of you; make sure your choice of rings reflects that in some way.

Since ancient times, the circle of the ring has symbolized eternity and wholeness: having no beginning or end. The Egyptians believed in the superstition that a vein ran from the fourth finger of the left hand directly to the heart. Since the heart controlled all of life and love, this finger was the most highly honored. It deserved the ring . . . the pledge of love. It's a wonderfully romantic thought that sums up the feelings that couples in love have for each other.

It's important for you to try to find a reputable jeweler who is a member of one of the legitimate gem institutes across the country. You will usually be able to find a wide selection of quality rings either in your favorite jewelry stores, or even online. While you're considering those options, don't rule out the idea of a family heirloom ring. An heirloom ring has history and usually unmatched stone quality. It makes a beautiful gift from your family and can be reset if it needs to be.

You may choose a style or type of ring that reflects your ancestral heritage. In certain Jewish traditions it is believed that the wedding ring should be completely plain, with no jewels or markings. This symbolizes eternal love—there's nothing to mark the beginning from the end. No "marred" breakage in the circle. An Irish wedding ring is called a

An Engagement Memory from the Inn

LOUISE CALLED ONE DAY TO ask if we were indeed a gay-friendly inn. The hostess told her not to worry, that we'd had several commitment ceremonies, and that we'd also been chosen one of the Top 12 Romantic Inns in the U.S., if she was worried about the inn having a romantic ambience. Louise decided to reserve a table outside in the gazebo among the roses—where she was planning to propose to Kathy.

She was very nervous on the phone as she made her reservation. She asked us to please not let on that we knew anything because it was a total surprise. We told her not to worry, that her table would be ready for her. She wanted our classical guitarist to be close by and asked if, as the dessert was served, he would play "La Vie En Rose." One of those wonderful and thoughtful touches that comes with some preplanning.

That night, after they were seated, Louise excused herself under the pretense of going to the restroom and stopped at the front desk, where I was standing beside the hostess. She pulled out a ring box, hardly able to speak, and she asked me to please put the diamond in "something apple" for dessert. "Apples are Kathy's favorite," she said. Luckily, it was fall and we had our chef Harry Swavely's warm apple crisp on the menu. Smiling from ear to ear, I assured her that we could handle this. Her parting words over her shoulder were "Oh God!" as she nervously went back to her table.

I went out to the kitchen and explained the assignment to Harry. I said that he had to set the ring somehow on top of the apple crisp, but I didn't want Kathy breaking her tooth on the damn thing so please to try and figure it out. I have never found out where Harry got it in the middle of the fall, but when I picked up the dessert, sitting on top of it was one of the most beautiful red roses I have ever seen in my life. The diamond had been placed lovingly in the center of it.

I planned to go over to the table, as nonchalantly as I could, and just place the dessert in front of Kathy. I walked out by the gazebo and approached the candlelit table, holding the dessert out in front of me. Kathy smiled at me as I brought it over. I sat it in front of her.

She looked at me with a nervous grin, looked over at Louise, and then back at me. I started to walk away. Kathy called out, "Excuse me." I looked at her and she said, "I'm sorry. I really don't want this!" I turned to look at Louise, who had turned the color of snow, and saw that her mouth was hanging open in shock. Louise looked at me and I knew that all of her hopes and dreams were being dashed in a single moment. Her life was being turned upside down. My mind was racing, and somehow—out of the blue, hoping against hope—I quickly said to Kathy, "Please, Louise really wants you to have this. Please. Just look at it, she wants you to have it." I began to walk away as Kathy looked down once again at the dessert.

All of a sudden, as I started back on the garden path, I heard this loud gasp . . . and then crying. I turned to see Louise down on her knees, pleadingly asking Kathy, "Will you? Will you?" And then I heard Kathy say through her tears, "Yes, for the rest of my life!" They began to hug and kiss, oblivious to everyone else.

You see, Kathy hadn't seen the ring, she'd just seen the dessert, and she was on a diet! Later on, during laughter and champagne for all, I told her never to do that again. I told her that she almost gave Louise—and me—a heart attack! Ah, proposals . . . no two are ever alike!

I will always remember Louise and Kathy, for their love and for allowing me to be a part of their special moment. It doesn't matter whether they're gay or straight, newly engaged couples are very special people who touch the lives of everyone lucky enough to be around them.

REMEMBER: *Love is love in all of its forms.*

Claddagh ring. It is a heart held by two hands with a crown. The hands represent faith, the crown symbolizes honor, and the heart signifies love. There are many traditions and many stone choices to make. Perhaps you might choose a Japanese pearl, a birthstone, or a stone of your favorite color set in both rings, thereby making them a matching set.

Whether you choose something old or something new, simple gold bands, solitaire diamond settings, or custom-made rings, don't just "settle" on something. Try to choose something that you both like, that you both will love to wear all the time, and a design that reflects your personal tastes.

If you are surprising your partner with a ring, consider a particular stone for the ring, one that they really love. If they love rubies and you love sapphires, consider having the same band with a different stone set for each of you.

If you happen to be picking out the ring on your own, and you're not sure of your partner's ring size, try to take one of their other rings into the jeweler to have the new ring sized so it will fit perfectly.

The metal in gold rings varies in color from yellow, to white, to platinum, to rose gold. Gold is available in 14, 18, or 24 carat. The term "carat" defines the quality and purity of the gold.

In ancient Greece, diamonds were considered teardrops of the gods, and it was believed that a diamond reflected the flames of love. Diamonds are judged on quality by the four Cs: cut, clarity, color, and carat. Each of these either adds or detracts from the value of the diamond. Each C affects reflected light in its own way.

Cut refers to the proportions and angles of the stone. Proportions and angles determine how light passes through the stone, creating the sparkle. We're talking bling, bling, baby! If diamonds are not cut to the right shape and proportion, the effects are less than optimal, even if it has great color and clarity.

Most diamonds range in color from clear to yellow, with clear being the best. To get a better idea of the color of a diamond, have your jeweler display the stone on white piece of paper. A black velvet pad can make a yellow diamond look clearer.

Clarity scale has eleven grades, though most differences can only be distinguished with a 10X microscope. In other words, a flawless diamond is no more beautiful to the unaided human eye than a grade in the middle of the scale. Subtle differences in clarity are very important to determine rarity, but only affect beauty when at the very low end of the scale. The easier flaws are to see, the worse the diamond is.

Carat weight is simply the weight of a diamond. While the weight of a diamond is important, a shallow-cut diamond will have a greater diameter, and will therefore look larger. A diamond with a superior cut will also look significantly larger than its actual size. Sometimes size doesn't matter!

The prong or claw setting is the most popular engagement setting for a variety of reasons. It consists of four or six claws that cradle the diamond and it allows the maximum amount of light to enter a stone from all angles. This makes the diamond appear larger and more brilliant. And it can hold large diamonds more securely.

Here are a few other settings to consider for diamonds and other gem stones:

CHANNEL SETTING: Most frequently for wedding and anniversary bands, a channel setting will set the stones right next to one another with no metal separating them. The outer ridge of metal is then worked over the edges of the stones.

BEZEL SETTING: A rim holds the stone and completely surrounds the gem.

GYPSY SETTING: The band is one continuous piece that gets thicker at the top. The top is shaped like a dome and the stone is inserted in the middle. There are no prongs, therefore the look is smooth and clean.

ILLUSION SETTING: More intricate than others in that it surrounds the stone to make it appear larger. The metal that surrounds the stone usually has an interesting design.

CLUSTER SETTING: Surrounds a larger center stone with several smaller stones. It is designed to create a beautiful larger ring from many smaller stones.

Determine which factors are most important to you and remember to keep in mind another C—cost. Stay within your budget! If you're not sure of what type of ring might be right for the two of you, make sure you look at a variety of styles and options from carefully selected jewelers.

Rings are a very personal matter, remember that. The two of you will be wearing them for a long time. My personal choice was to have my partner involved in making the decision. We ended up with platinum and gold with a central diamond. Personally speaking, it could have been one of the cigar bands for all I cared. It was the intention behind it that really carried the weight for me. But hey, I've grown to love the ring. Those diamonds really do sparkle, don't they?

Letting Your Family Know

"Our love isn't just some sentimental feeling, it's a commitment. It doesn't just happen . . . it's a choice we both make."

LOUISE

We aren't going to try to kid you here. Being gay or lesbian, you already know the reactions will vary widely when you decide to tell others of your upcoming wedding plans. Announcing nuptials can either bring out the best or the worst in people, especially when it comes to family.

If you're doing your wedding privately, you will probably keep it to yourself, or tell just a close-knit circle of carefully selected friends or family. Don't agonize over this too much. We have some guidelines to help you through this part, should you decide to let more people know about your plans. If you're totally out and could care less what any prejudiced or narrow-minded people think, our hats are off to you. But please, be sure your intended feels the same way you do before you take out an engagement announcement in your local newspaper! It's only fair that they should play a part in this important decision-making process.

The bottom line about your wedding is that it is *your* wedding, together as a couple, not anyone else's.

The ceremony, in whatever form it takes, is a meaningful and often spiritual event. Never let anyone stand between the two of you and your heartfelt intentions.

The main point of all of this is, when you decide to tell family and friends, don't expect everyone to understand and to applaud you. If there isn't any way to educate them and they make that plain to you, then leave it alone. Don't let their prejudices spoil your memories of this special occasion.

With that in mind, here are some tips for announcing your engagement:

+ Start with those you care about the most, the people in your life who have been the most supportive of the two of you. (By the way, some of these particular friends and family will probably be the ones you will want to be members of your wedding party. They can help you tremendously if you let them share some of the responsibility.)

+ If you don't feel like explaining . . . don't! (But remember, this is your chance to educate people about the importance of benefits, rights, and equality in a non-aggressive and personal way.)

+ If you haven't ever told your family that you are gay, you know this will come as a bit of a shock to them, to say the least. When you add to that your announcement of impending nuptials, you may have to get out the smelling salts! Have compassion here. If you care about these people, give them time and space to digest the news. If you're spiritual, say a little prayer for them so they can have understanding and eventually come around!

Unless you tell people, you will never know how they feel. It's so much easier for uneducated people to say, "I hear queers are getting married now." It's a whole 'nother story to hear that "Bobby and Brett, my cousin, have decided to get married." Don't try to cause extra dramas if you don't need to, but at the same time, don't back down on who you are and what your partner means to you unless you absolutely have to. Given time, it may also be a little easier for family members to accept and come to the understanding that you have had for a while.

You can't, though, ever live your lives in fear and shame. Finding someone special to share your life with goes beyond explanation. If you get disapproval from some, you may want to consider how much you really need those people in your life. (But again, we suggest that you give them time to feel their way through this, especially if they are important people in your lives.)

As we begin to show more and more positive, committed, meaningful gay role models to the world, we work toward more acceptance for all of us. Remember, your commitment and relationship to each other can, in its own small way, help to make the world a much more accepting and loving place!

Newspaper Announcements

Obviously, word will spread quickly about your upcoming nuptials among family and friends. The question is whether or not you want to put your announcement in your local newspaper. Many publications are now beginning to list gay and lesbian weddings, so don't automatically assume that they won't include yours, especially in a metropolitan area.

You should get in touch with the lifestyle editor at a newspaper. Usually this section comes out (no pun intended here) once a week. Call the paper if you and your partner both agree to do this, and see what their deadline and requirements are. Also ask whether or not they accept photos. Ask them if there will be any charge and have them fax or email you a form to fill out. Find out if you should drop off the form and picture at the newspaper in person, or if it's possible to save yourself a trip by emailing the information. Email any photos in a high-resolution format. Your announcement should be double spaced for editing purposes. Look at other announcements in the newspaper to see how they're worded.

Traditional wedding books recommend that you place the announcements in the communities where your parents live also. That advice you might definitely want to take with a grain of salt! As much as my mother may love me, putting my announcement in her local paper would have freaked her out, to say the least, if I hadn't first given her a heads-up or allowed her to soften the news by telling her friends first. At least with my mother, it all boils down to a matter of courtesy, not a political statement in this regard.

After looking over some examples of announcements, you'll have a good idea of what to write. Include some information about your and your partner's work backgrounds if you want, the schools you've attended, and when and where you plan to have your ceremony. There are various ways to word the announcement. The announcement can be made by parents, a family member, a close friend, or by the two of you:

Ms. Dawn Somers announces the engagement of her sister,

Dina Somers, to Mary Johnson

OR

Tim Ward and Michael Nelson announce their upcoming

nuptials to each other.

It is critical that neither of you allows this to become a point of contention between the two of you, whether to make a public announcement. Partners should both agree that they want to make this sort of public written announcement to be put in the newspapers. If your partner doesn't like the idea, the last thing you want to do is force the issue upon them without good cause.

For a list of gay-friendly newspapers around the country that will post your announcement, consult the Human Rights Campaign website (www.HRC.org). This website is also a great resource if your partner has decided to come out but is unsure of the best first steps.

Here are some newspapers across the country that publish same-sex union announcements (Source: GLAAD's Announcing Equality Project):

Alabama
The Burmingham News (Birmingham, AL)
Demopolis Times (Demopolis, AL)
Enterprise Ledger (Enterprise, AL)
Montgomery Advertiser (Montgomery, AL)
Opelika-Auburn News (Opelika, AL)
The Tuscaloosa News (Tuscaloosa, AL)

Alaska
Anchorage Daily News (Anchorage, AK)
The Juneau Empire (Juneau, AK)
Kodiak Daily Mirror (Kodiak, AK)
Daily Sitka Sentinel (Sitka, AK)

Arizona
Mohave Valley Daily News (Bullhead City, AZ)
Casa Grande Dispatch (Casa Grande, AZ)
The Daily Dispatch (Douglas, AZ)
East Valley Tribune (Mesa, AZ)
Arizona Republic (Phoenix, AZ)
Daily News-Sun (Sun City, AZ)
Arizona Daily Star (Tucson, AZ)
Tucson Citizen (Tucson, AZ)
The Yuma Daily Sun (Yuma, AZ)

Arkansas
Batesville Guard (Batesville, AR)
Southwest Times Record (Fort Smith, AR)
The Daily Citizen (Searcy, AR)

California
El Mexicano (Bonita, CA)
The Hanford Sentinel (Hanford, CA)
The Daily Review (Hayward, CA)
The Modesto Bee (Modesto, CA)
Bakersfield Californian (Bakersfield, CA)
Desert Dispatch (Barstow, CA)
Davis Enterprise (Davis, CA)
North County Times (Escondido, CA)
The Times-Standard (Eureka, CA)
Lake County Record Bee (Lakeport, CA)
San Diego Jewish Times (La Mesa, CA)
The Press-Telegram (Long Beach, CA)
La Opinión (Los Angeles, CA)
Los Angeles Times (Los Angeles, CA)
Appeal-Democrat (Marysville, CA)
The Napa Valley Register (Napa, CA)
Marin Independent Journal (Novato, CA)
The Oakland Tribune (Oakland, CA)
Inland Valley Daily Bulletin (Ontario, CA)
Mercury-Register (Oroville, CA)

The d (Palm Desert, CA)

Desert Sun (Palm Springs, CA)

Palo Alto Weekly (Palo Alto, CA)

Argus Courier (Petaluma, CA)

The Tri-Valley Herald (Pleasanton, CA)

Porterville Recorder (Porterville, CA)

Record Searchlight (Redding, CA)

West County Times (Richmond, CA)

Daily Independent (Ridgecrest, CA)

The Press-Enterprise (Riverside, CA)

The Sacramento Bee (Sacramento, CA)

The Salinas Californian
(Sacramento, CA)

San Bernardino County Sun
(San Bernardino, CA)

Union Tribune (San Diego, CA)

San Francisco Chronicle
(San Francisco, CA)

Jewish Bulletin of Northern California
(San Francisco, CA)

San Jose Mercury News (San Jose, CA)

The Tribune (San Luis Obispo, CA)

Orange County Register
(Santa Ana, CA)

News-Press (Santa Barbara, CA)

Santa Cruz Sentinel (Santa Cruz, CA)

Santa Monica Press Daily
(Santa Monica, CA)

Press Democrat (Santa Rosa, CA)

Tahoe Daily Tribune
(South Lake Tahoe, CA)

The Record (Stockton, CA)

The Daily Breeze (Torrance, CA)

Ukiah Daily Journal (Ukiah, CA)

The Signal & Saugus Enterprise
(Valencia, CA)

Vallejo Times-Herald (Vallejo, CA)

Ventura County Star (Ventura, CA)

Daily Press (Victorville, CA)

Contra Costa Times
(Walnut Creek, CA)

San Gabriel Valley Tribune
(West Covina, CA)

Whittier Daily News (Whittier, CA)

The Daily Democrat (Woodland, CA)

Daily News (Woodland Hills, CA)

Siskiyou Daily News (Yreka, CA)

Colorado

Aspen Times (Aspen, CO)

Daily Camera (Boulder, CO)

The Gazette (Colorado Springs, CO)

Rocky Mountain News (Denver, CO)

Denver Post (Denver, CO)

The Coloradoan (Ft. Collins, CO)

La Junta Tribune-Democrat
(La Junta, CO)

Lamar Daily News (Lamar, CO)

Pueblo Chieftain (Pueblo, CO)

Rocky Ford Daily Gazette
(Rocky Ford, CO)

Steamboat Pilot & Today
(Steamboat, CO)

Journal Advocate (Sterling, CO)

The Chronicle News (Trinidad, CO)

Connecticut

Bridgeport News (Bridgeport, CT)

The Bristol News (Bristol, CT)

The News Times (Danbury, CT)

Hartford Courant (Hartford, CT)

The Journal Inquirer (Manchester, CT)

New Haven Register (New Haven, CT)

The Day (New London, CT)

Norwich Bulletin (Norwich, CT)

The Advocate (Stamford, CT)

The Register Citizen (Torrington, CT)

Delaware

Delaware State News (Dover, DE)

The News Journal (New Castle, DE)

District of Columbia

Washington Post (Washington, DC)

Florida

Bradenton Herald (Bradenton, FL)

The News-Journal (Daytona Beach, FL)

The Destin Log (Destin, FL)

Sun-Sentinel (Ft. Lauderdale, FL)

N'west Daily Florida News
(Ft. Walton Beach, FL)

The Citizen (Key West, FL)

The Ledger (Lakeland, FL)

Jackson County Floridan (Marianna, FL)

Miami Herald (Miami, FL)

The Daily Okeechobee News
(Okeechobee, FL)

Orlando Sentinel (Orlando, FL)

Palm Beach Daily News (Palm Beach, FL)

The News Herald (Panama City, FL)

St. Petersburg Times (St. Petersburg, FL)

Walton Sun (Santa Rosa Beach, FL)

Tallahassee Democrat (Tallahassee, FL)

The Tampa Tribune (Tampa, FL)

The Palm Beach Post
(West Palm Beach, FL)

Georgia

Atlanta Journal-Constitution
(Atlanta, GA)

Columbus Ledger-Enquirer
(Columbus, GA)

Trib Publications, Inc. (Fayetteville, GA)

La Vision (Lawrenceville, GA)

Marietta Daily Journal (Marietta, GA)

Daily Herald (McDonough, GA)

Hawaii

Honolulu Advertiser (Honolulu, HI)

The Maui News (Wailuku, HI)

Idaho

Coeur D'Alene Press
(Coeur D'Alene, ID)

Post Register (Idaho Falls, ID)

Shoshone News Press (Kellogg, ID)

Lewiston Morning Tribune (Lewiston, ID)

Illinois

The Telegraph (Alton, IL)

The Daily Herald (Arlington Heights, IL)

Beacon News (Aurora, IL)

The Benton Evening News (Benton, IL)

Chicago Tribune (Chicago, IL)

Chicago Sun-Times (Chicago, IL)

Red Streak (Chicago, IL)

The Courier News (Elgin, IL)

Daily Register (Harrisburg, IL)

Jacksonville Journal-Courier
(Jacksonville, IL)

Daily Record (Lawrenceville, IL)

The Courier (Lincoln, IL)

Litchfield News-Herald (Litchfield, IL)

Macomb Journal (Macomb, IL)

Journal Gazette (Mattoon, IL)

Daily Review Atlas (Monmouth, IL)

The Register News (Mount Vernon, IL)

The Daily Leader (Pontiac, IL)

Rockford Register Star (Rockford, IL)

Iroquois Times-Republic (Watseka, IL)

The News-Sun (Waukegan, IL)

Indiana

Herald Bulletin (Anderson, IN)

Herald-Republican (Angola, IN)

The Herald Times (Bloomington, IN)

The Elkhart Truth (Elkhart, IN)

The Journal Gazette (Fort Wayne, IN)

Huntington Herald Press
(Huntington, IN)

The Star Press (Muncie, IN)

The Tribune (New Albany, IN)

Noblesville Daily Times (Noblesville, IN)

Rensselaer Republican (Rensselaer, IN)

Sullivan Daily Times (Sullivan, IN)

Tipton Tribune (Tipton, IN)

The News Gazette (Winchester, IN)

Iowa

The Tribune (Ames, IA)

The Hawk Eye (Burlington, IA)

The Gazette (Cedar Rapids, IA)

Centerville Daily Iowegian
(Centerville, IA)

The Des Moines Register
(Des Moines, IA)

Telegraph Herald (Dubuque, IA)

Iowa City Press-Citizen (Iowa City, IA)

Mount Pleasant News
(Mount Pleasant, IA)

Oelwein Daily Register (Oelwein, IA)

Valley News Today (Shenandoah, IA)

Courier (Waterloo, IA)

Kansas

Clay Center Dispatch (Clay Center, KS)

Coffeeville Journal (Coffeeville, KS)

Colby Free Press (Colby, KS)

Columbus Daily Advocate
(Columbus, KS)

Concordia Blade-Empire
(Concordia, KS)

Council Grove Republican
(Council Grove, KS)

Lyons Daily News (Lyons, KS)

McPherson Sentinel (McPherson, KS)

Salina Journal (Salina, KS)

Wichita Eagle (Wichita, KS)

Kentucky

Corbin Times-Tribune (Corbin, KY)

The State Journal (Frankfort, KY)

The Harlan Daily Enterprise
(Harlan, KY)

Kentucky New Era (Hopkinsville, KY)

Louisville Courier-Journal (Louisville, KY)

The Ledger Independent (Maysville, KY)

Louisiana

Franklin Banner-Tribune (Jennings, LA)

The Daily Review (Morgan city, LA)

Natchitoches Times (Natchitoches, LA)

The Daily Iberian (New Iberia, LA)

Times-Picayune (New Orleans, LA)

Daily World (Opelousas, LA)

Maine

Kennebec Journal (Augusta, ME)

Bangor Daily News (Bangor, ME)

Journal Tribune (Biddeford, ME)

The Times Record (Brunswick, ME)

Sun Journal (Lewiston, ME)

Portland Press Herald (Portland, ME)

Morning Sentinel (Waterville, ME)

Maryland

The Sun (Baltimore, MD)

The Daily Banner (Cambridge, MD)

The Star Democrat (Easton, MD)

Cecil Whig (Elkton, MD)

The Daily Times (Salisbury, MD)

Massachusetts

Athol Daily News (Athol, MA)

The Sun Chronicle (Attleboro, MA)

Bolton Common (Bolton, MA)

Boston Globe (Boston, MA)

Boston Herald (Boston, MA)

The Enterprise (Brockton, MA)

Cambridge Chronicle (Cambridge, MA)

The Herald News (Fall River, MA)

Sentinel & Enterprise (Fitchburg, MA)

MetroWest Daily News
(Framingham, MA)

Gloucester Daily Times
(Gloucester, MA)

Greenfield Recorder (Greenfield, MA)

Cape Cod Times (Hyannis, MA)

The Sun (Lowell, MA)

The Daily Item (Lynn, MA)

The Melrose Free Press (Melrose, MA)

The Standard-Times (New Bedford, MA)

Daily Hampshire Gazette
(Northampton, MA)

Daily News (Newburyport, MA)

The Cape Codder (Orleans, MA)

Berkshire Eagle (Pittsfield, MA)

Provincetown Banner
(Provincetown, MA)

The Patriot-Ledger (Quincy, MA)

Taunton Daily Gazette (Taunton, MA)

Westfield Evening News (Westfield, MA)

Telegram & Gazette (Worcester, MA)

Michigan

Ann Arbor News (Ann Arbor, MI)

Battle Creek Enquirer (Battle Creek, MI)

Pioneer (Big Rapids, MI)

Cheboygan Tribune (Cheboygan, MI)

Detroit News (Detroit, MI)

Flint Journal (Flint, MI)

Livingston County Daily Press
(Howell, MI)

The Daily News (Iron Mountain, MI)

The Lansing State Journal (Lansing, MI)

Kalamazoo Gazette (Kalamazoo, MI)

Manistee News-Advocate (Manistee, MI)

The Oakland Press (Oakland, MI)

Petoskey News-Review (Petoskey, MI)

Times Herald (Port Huron, MI)

The Daily Tribune (Royal Oak, MI)

The Saginaw News (Saginaw, MI)

Sturgis Journal (Sturgis, MI)

Minnesota

Albert Lea Tribune (Albert Lea, MN)

Duluth News Tribune, (Duluth, MN)

Minneapolis Star Tribune
(Minneapolis, MN)

Stillwater Gazette (Stillwater, MN)

The St. Paul Pioneer Press (St. Paul, MN)

Missouri

Columbia Daily Tribune (Columbia, MO)

Columbia Missourian (Columbia, MO)

The Examiner (Independence, MO)

The Daily Dunkin Democrat
(Kennett, MO)

Lebanon Daily Record (Lebanon, MO)

The Daily Journal (Park Hills, MO)

Jewish Light (St. Louis, MO)

St. Louis Post-Dispatch (St. Louis, MO)

Daily Guide (St. Robert, MO)

Sedalia Democrat (Sedalia, MO)

Montana

The Missoluian (Missoula, MT)

Nebraska

Alliance Times-Herald (Alliance, NE)

Lincoln Journal Star (Lincoln, NE)

McCook Daily Gazette (McCook, NE)

Nevada

Reno Gazette Journal (Reno, NV)

New Hampshire

Berlin Daily Sun (Berlin, NH)

Concord Monitor (Concord, NH)

Foster's Daily Democrat (Dover, NH)

The Telegraph (Hudson, NH)

Keene Sentinel (Keene, NH)

The Conway Daily Sun
(North Conway, NH)

Monadnock Ledger (Peterborough, NH)

Valley News (West Lebanon, NH)

New Jersey

The Courier-News (Bridgewater, NJ)

Home News Tribune
(East Brunswick, NJ)

The Record (Hackensack, NJ)

Jersey Journal (Jersey City, NJ)

Asbury Park Press (Neptune, NJ)

Star-Ledger (Newark, NJ)

The Press of Atlantic City
(Pleasantville, NJ)

Ocean County Observer
(Toms River, NJ)

The Trentonian (Trenton, NJ)

The Daily Journal (Vineland, NJ

New Mexico

Clovis News-Journal (Clovis, NM)

Portales News-Tribune (Portales, NM)

The Quay County Sun (Tucumcari, NM)

New York

Times-Union (Albany, NY)

Brooklyn Daily Eagle (Brooklyn, NY)

Buffalo News (Buffalo, NY)

The Daily Messenger (Canadaigua, NY)

Corning Leader (Corning, NY)

East Hampton Independent (East
Hampton, NY)

East Hampton Star (East Hampton, NY)

Leader-Herald (Gloversville, NY)

Ithaca Journal (Ithaca, NY)

The Post-Journal (Jamestown, NY)

The Daily Freeman (Kingston, NY)

Times Herald Record (Middletown, NY)

New York Observer (New York, NY)

The New York Times (New York, NY)

The Evening Sun (Norwich, NY)

Press-Republican (Plattsburgh, NY)

Democrat & Chronicle (Rochester, NY)

Adirondack Enterprise
(Saranac Lake, NY)

The Saratogian (Saratoga, NY)

Staten Island Advance (Staten Island, NY)

The Record (Troy, NY)

Daily Sentinel (Utica, NY)

Observer-Dispatch (Utica, NY)

Press & Sun-Bulletin (Vestal, NY)

Watertown Daily Times
(Watertown, NY)

Wellsville (Wellsville, NY)

The Humboldt Sun (Winnemucca, NY)

The Yonkers Tribune (Yonkers, NY)

North Carolina

Asheville Citizen Times (Asheville, NC)

Times-News (Burlington, NC)

Charlotte Observer (Charlotte, NC)

The Daily Advance (Ellizabeth City, NC)

Fayetteville Observer (Fayetteville, NC)

Gaston Gazette (Gastonia, NC)

Havelock News (Havelock, NC)

The Hickory News (Hickory, NC)

The Daily News (Jacksonville, NC)

The Free Press (Kinston, NC)

Sun Journal (New Bern, NC)

The News & Observer (Raleigh, NC)

The Shelby Star (Shelby, NC)

Winston Salem Journal (Winston, NC)

North Dakota
The Forum (Fargo, ND)

Grand Forks Herald (Grand Forks, ND)

Ohio
The Akron Beacon Journal (Akron, OH)

The Alliance Review (Alliance, OH)

Sentinel-Tribune (Bowling Green, OH)

Cincinnati Enquirer (Cincinnati, OH)

Plain Dealer (Cleveland, OH)

Columbus Dispatch (Columbus, OH)

The Lima News (Lima, OH)

Port Clinton News Herald (Port Clinton, OH)

Record-Courier (Ravenna, OH)

Record-Herald
(Wash. Court House, OH)

Oklahoma
Norman Transcript (Norman, OK)

Oregon
Albany Democrat-Herald (Albany, OR)

Ashland Daily Tidings (Ashland, OR)

Beaverton Valley Times (Beaverton, OR)

Argus Observer (Ontario, OR)

The Oregonian (Portland, OR)

Willamette Week (Portland, OR)

The Statesman Journal (Salem, OR)

Tigard Times (Tigard, OR)

Tualatin Times (Tualatin, OR)

Pennsylvania
Beaver County Times (Beaver, PA)

Press-Enterprise (Bloomsburg, PA)

The Sentinel (Carlisle, PA)

The Daily Courier (Connellsville, PA)

Danville News (Danville, PA)

The Intelligencer (Doylestown, PA)

The Courier-Express (DuBois, PA)

The Express-Times (Easton, PA)

Ellwood City Ledger (Ellwood City, PA)

The Patriot-News (Harrisburg, PA)

The Wayne Independent (Honesdale, PA)

The Reporter (Lansdale, PA)

Daily News (Lebanon, PA)

The Times News (Lehighton, PA)

Bucks County Courier Times
(Levittown, PA)

The Express (Lock Haven, PA)

The Meadville Tribune (Meadville, PA)

The Derrick (Oil City, PA)

Philadelphia Daily News
(Philadelphia, PA)

Philadelphia Inquirer (Philadelphia, PA)

The Phoenix (Phoenixville, PA)

Pittsburgh Post Gazette (Pittsburgh, PA)

Delaware County Daily Times
(Primos, PA)

Daily Press (Saint Marys, PA)

The Herald (Sharon, PA)

Centre Daily Times (State College, PA)

Pocono Record (Stroudsburg, PA)

Valley News Dispatch (Tarentum, PA)

Warren Times Observer (Warren, PA)

Observer-Reporter (Washington, PA)

York Daily Record (York, PA)

York Dispatch (York, PA)

Rhode Island

Newport Daily News (Newport, RI)

Providence Journal (Providence, RI)

Warwick Beacon (Warwick, RI)

Kent County Daily Times
(West Warwick, RI)

The Westerly Sun (Westerly, RI)

South Carolina

The Sun News (Myrtle Beach, SC)

South Dakota

Huron Plainsman (Huron, SD)

Tennessee

The Leaf-Chronicle (Clarksville, TN)

Johnson City Press (Johnson City, TN)

Kingsport Times-News (Kingsport, TN)

The Nashville Tennessean (Nashville, TN)

Texas

Abilene Reporter-News (Abilene, TX)

Austin American-Statesman (Austin, TX)

Athens Daily Review (Athens, TX)

Brownsville Herald (Brownsville, TX)

Corpus Christi Caller-Times
(Corpus Christi, TX)

Dallas Morning News (Dallas, TX)

Del Rio News-Herald (Del Rio, TX)

Denton Record-Chronicle (Denton, TX)

Focus Daily News (Desoto, TX)

The News Gram (Eagle Press, TX)

Diario de Juarez (El Paso, TX)

El Paso Times (El Paso, TX)

Ennis Daily News (Ennis, TX)

Valley Morning Star (Harlngen, TX)

Houston Chronicle (Houston, TX)

Korea Times-Houston (Houston, TX)

Huntsville Item (Huntsville, TX)

Jacksonville Daily Progress
(Jacksonville, TX)

Laredo Morning Times (Laredo, TX)

Noticias En Espanol (Laredo, TX)

The Monitor (McAllen, TX)

McKinney Courier-Gazette
(McKinney, TX)

Odessa American (Odessa, TX)

The Paris News (Paris, TX)

Pecos Enterprise (Pecos, TX)

San Antonio Express News (San
Antonio, TX)

San Marcos Daily Record
(San Marcos, TX)

Seguin Gazette-Enterprise (Seguin, TX)

Taylor Press (Taylor, TX)

Waxahachie Daily Light
(Waxahachie, TX)

The Mid-Valley Town Crier
(Weslaco, TX)

Utah

Southern Utah News (Kanab, UT)

Herald Journal (Logan, UT)

Deseret Morning News
(Salt Lake City, UT)

Salt Lake Tribune (Salt Lake City, UT)

Vermont

The Times Argus (Barre, VT)

Bennington Banner (Bennington, VT)

The Brattleboro Reformer
(Brattleboro, VT)

Burlington Free Press (Burlington, VT)

Newport Daily Express (Newport, VT)

The Rutland Herald (Rutland, VT)

St. Albans Messenger (Saint Albans, VT)

The Caledonian-Record
(Saint Johnsburg, VT)

Virginia

The News Leader (Staunton, VA)

Falls Church News-Press
(Falls Church, VA)

Hopewell News (Hopewell, VA)

Northern Virginia Daily (Strasburg, VA)

The Roanoke Times (Roanoke, VA)

Washington

Eastside Journal (Bellevue, WA)

Bellingham Herald (Bellingham, WA)

The Chronicle (Centralia, WA)

Daily Record (Ellensburg, WA)

Everett Herald (Everett, WA)

The Olympian (Olympia, WA)

Seattle Times (Seattle, WA)

Ballard News-Tribune (Seattle, WA)

Korea Times-Seattle (Seattle, WA)

Seattle Post-Intelligencer (Seattle, WA)

The Spokesman Review (Spokane, WA)

News Tribune (Tacoma, WA)

Walla Walla Union-Bulletin
(Walla Walla, WA)

Wenatchee World (Wenatchee, WA)

West Virginia

Charleston Daily Mail (Charleston, WV)

The Charleston Gazette
(Charleston, WV)

The Inter-Mountain (Elkins, WV)

West Virginia Daily News
(Lewisburg, WV)

The Logan Banner (Logan, WV)

Point Pleasant Register
(Point Pleasant, WV)

Wisconsin

The Appleton Post-Crescent
(Appleton, WI)

The Daily Press (Ashland, WI)

Chippewa Herald (Chippewa Falls, WI)

Leader-Telegram (Eau Claire, WI)

Green Bay News-Chronicle
(Green Bay, WI)

Press-Gazette (Green Bay, WI)

Kenosha News (Kenosha, WI)

Capital Times (Madison, WI)

Wisconsin State Journal (Madison, WI)

Eagle Herald (Marinette, WI)

Marshfield News-Herald (Marshfield, WI)

Milwaukee Journal-Sentinel
(Milwaukee, WI)

Oshkosh Northwestern (Oshkosh, WI)

The Journal Times (Racine, WI)

Sheboygan Press (Sheboygan, WI)

Stevens Point Journal (Stevens Point, WI)

Daily Telegram (Superior, WI)

The Daily Tribune
(Wisconsin Rapids, WI)

The Daily News (West Bend, WI)

Wausau Daily Herald (Wausau, WI)

Wyoming

Casper Star-Tribune (Casper, WY)

Tribune-Eagle (Cheyenne, WY)

Laramie Boomerang (Laramie, WY)

Daily Rocket Miner (Rock Springs, WY)

Sheridan Press (Sheridan, WY)

Planning and Organization

The Basic Tips

"I was so proud of myself, how organized I kept everything all the way up to the wedding. My partner couldn't believe how beautifully it all came together. That is, until we were about to walk up the aisle together. I wasn't paying attention to how badly I had to go to the bathroom until the very last minute and I ran off, leaving her standing there. She thought I was leaving her at the altar!"

HELEN

If you want to have an affair to remember, the most important thing to do, besides using your imagination and creativity, is to keep all of the wedding stuff you're accumulating organized. Remember that no event, especially a wedding, will ever be totally perfect no matter how much you try. There will always be little things that will not go your way. But if you stay organized, both of you will learn quickly that organization goes a long way in helping to keep things running smoothly.

Here are a few great tips to keep yourself on the right track as you start your planning:

1. Buy a large briefcase of some kind to keep everything relating to the wedding in. Make sure that it has your address and phone somewhere on it at all times—the last thing you ever want to do is to lose it! Keep everything about your wedding stored inside, including phone numbers; notebooks with ideas written in them; a calendar with appointments; contracts; receipts; menus; pictures from vendors, etc.

    *   Keep a notebook or date book made for you and your attendants. List their specific duties, dates for fittings, rehearsal times, any further research that needs to be done, etc.

    *   Keep a separate large notebook also, in which both you and your partner can list important details. Include various important dates like going to see the rehearsal hall, fittings, or meetings with your caterer. Keep it organized at all times so it's very clear where you're at with everything.

2. When you or your partner feel your stress level getting high, turn to our chapter about dealing with stress. Take time to unwind if you need to. Once you feel balanced again, get back to the task at hand in a calm fashion. Everything should be broken up into small steps whenever possible. This will make everything seem much more manageable as you go along.

3. Don't put off today what you can do today. Make those phone calls and decisions and don't procrastinate or leave things on the back burner. Use our "Your Wedding Checklist" chapter to keep your plans in line with all of your goals.

4. Be sure to use the help of your support team and attendants whenever you can. Take them up on their offers to help. Don't feel like you're taking advantage of them if they are offering. Give detailed directions whenever possible. Make sure they let you know if they run into obstacles of any kind. Be sure to give everybody as many of the details as they need to get the job

done the way you need it to be done. Sometimes not describing what it is you're after, in great detail, can cause you major headaches later on, so be descriptive about what it is you're looking for. Be sure also to get your partner involved, in case there's only one of you who'll be handling most of the details. Find jobs they enjoy doing and that will involve them in the planning. It will help you and, at the same time, they'll feel useful.

5. Remember one very important word for you to keep in mind as you get busy with all of this. That key word is *flexibility*. Without flexibility, you could cause yourself a lot of unnecessary heartache if, for instance, you can't afford that perfect cake or if the perfect flowers are out of season. And for God's sake, don't lose friendships over the small, unimportant matters. Try to keep your emotions from running wild when you start to deal with (what seems like) thousands of details.

6. Try to set a weekly time for you and your partner, as a couple, to get together over the details. Make it as consistent as possible by having the meeting on the same day every week. It's a good idea to try to meet in a comfortable place, one that you can both enjoy. It could be over coffee at your neighborhood café or lunch at your favorite restaurant—anywhere you can find a quiet table where you can concentrate on the details and just enjoy the pleasure of each other's company without a lot of added pressure. This will help you to establish a regular weekly rhythm. Meet more often if you need to, but always end the meeting on an upbeat note that will keep you in good spirits for what's to come.

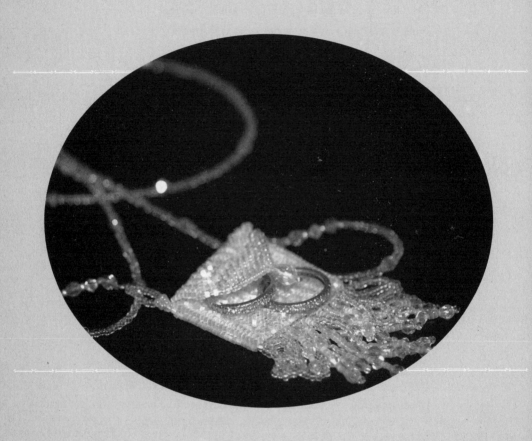

Your Budget

"*I will always remember the line that was said during the vows that made me start crying. She had written the words herself. 'Even if the stars in heaven should grow cold, I give you my promise, from my heart and soul, that I will love you forever . . . no matter what lies ahead.' I knew, as she was saying it, that she was promising that right from her soul to mine.*"

HOLLY

This is the chapter that no one enjoys. My staff and I are in total agreement that talking about a budget gives us all a major headache. How does one go about trying to figure out what a wedding is going to cost in the long run?

It was fairly easy when we were offering Complete Wedding Packages for Two at our inns across the country on the GayWeddings.com website. Larger weddings we usually directed to our sister site, GayWeddingPlanners.com, where couples could try to find a wedding planner in their home state. At the inn we owned, we offered a per-person charge that would or would not include the bar and drinks, depending on the package. The rest was left up to the couple.

Ultimately, costs will be a determining factor in how large a wedding you will have, what type of place you can have it in, how elaborate your decorations will be, and what you'll serve at the reception.

We want to try to keep this as simple as possible for both of you. Know that it is the formal and upscale venues that obviously will cost the most. Before we start to spend your money, though, there are a few things to keep in mind that could help you to cut a few corners. Consider them as you watch the dollars add up.

If you are two of those lucky, lucky people for whom cost is no concern whatsoever then please skip down past this part. But even you, too, might enjoy the idea of saving a little money for that next Rothko or a quick buying spree on the Via Napolioni in Milan.

⊢——⊣

Setting Your Budget
Some Little Cost Savers That Really Add Up

✦ Remember that booking certain places at the height of "high season" is going to cost you more.

✦ June and July are the most popular wedding months in the country and usually considered "high season." High season is different if you are looking to marry in Vermont, where the prime months are during fall foliage and winter ski season. The location of your venue will determine the high season and bargain season.

✦ Having your wedding on a Saturday night will cost much more than having the affair on a Friday night or Sunday afternoon.

✦ Dinner is always more expensive than having a brunch; people also drink less at brunch!

✦ Sit-down dinner is more costly than a buffet.

+ Offering steak as a choice of entrée will cost you more than chicken, lamb, or duck (see our menu section).

+ As far as music goes, a band (no matter what combination you have) is going to cost you a lot more than a classical guitarist, harpist, keyboard player, or DJ.

+ Having your affair in a major city is more costly than having it in a smaller hometown.

+ Computer programs and companies like Staples can do your print work for much less than stationery companies.

+ One of the biggest money savers is to cut down on the outgoing number of invitations. In other words, downsize! A big cost-cutter is having an adults-only affair. Almost all of our weddings at the inn have been for guests over sixteen; the couples loved it because it cost them less and they could blame it on us!

+ Cut down on mailings and stamps by having your guests email or phone in RSVPs.

+ Consider having your ceremony and reception at the same place. It cuts down on double decorating, car services, and many other services.

+ Only serve wine with dinner and a champagne cocktail (our recipe) beforehand for the toast. The alcohol bill is always one of the greatest expenses and this will cut the per-person charge down tremendously. An alternative, almost nearly as effective, is to have an open bar for only one hour of cocktails, then begin the wine pouring at the tables. Not only is this tremendously cost effective, but you also don't have to worry as much about people drinking and driving home.

+ Instead of using straight champagne—no pun intended—try having your location make champagne cocktails; they're great and cost much less than regular champagnes! (See our menus section.)

+ Don't pick the highest-priced hors d'oeuvres on the menu. Ask if the location can make tomatoes filled with humus, or cucumber sandwiches, or even paté—a great alternative to higher-priced counterparts.

+ Renting your outfits is definitely less expensive than buying, so consider this as an option, or shop for beautiful vintage bargains that you can be proud that you found—they do exist!

- ✦ Flowers offer major cost savings if you have talented friends and resources such as a beautiful perennial garden from which you can pick and create. We have done many a wedding at the inn where all the flowers and roses came from our own gardens and cost almost nothing for our couples.

- ✦ Remember, if you are on an ultra-tight budget, but the two of you love each other and want this wedding really badly, all it takes is your love, a house and garden (with a tent in case it rains), and some great friends who can cook and who want to help you both have one heck of a celebration. We've been to a few of those, too, and had a great time!

- ✦ It's important not to forget to research and network through your attendants, friends, and family. Tell them you're budgeting if you have to, but more importantly, tell them you need their creative ideas. You'll be surprised how many incredible cost-saving ideas can come your way through these wonderful folks you're lucky enough to know.

- ✦ We hate to suggest it, but if you are really thinking of cutting costs, one of the easiest ways to achieve this is by forgetting that dream-of-a-lifetime honeymoon and take off for a few days to a more affordable romantic retreat nearby. It's cheaper and much easier to take a car or train into the country or the city (depending on your preference).

But listen . . . if there's any way you can still plan that paradise honeymoon, try to cut the costs in other ways, okay? Those family and friends who love you are there to help. Trust in that as much as you can!

The traditional ways of paying for a wedding don't really work, generally speaking, for us gay couples. Why? Well, for example, I can just see telling my mom that she's going to be considered the mother of the bride and asking for a blank check. Trust me, that would not make her happy, and quite frankly, it wouldn't make me happy either! My sister would probably argue that it wasn't fair because old stereotypes about straight couples don't work when it comes to gay and lesbian relationships and weddings. So the question becomes, who's going to be paying for what?

And our answer to that, after doing all of the gay and lesbian weddings we have done, is: "Whoever you can get, that's who!"

Seriously though, we think that most couples end up paying for most of the ceremony and reception by themselves. Sometimes the two families will divvy it up among themselves as fairly as they can. We love it when that happens! We think it should have always been that way, even before families of gay and lesbian couples started doing this. How many families of traditional brides went broke trying to go beyond their means? That's sad and unfair when you think about it.

One of the upsides of paying for your own wedding is that neither set of parents can raise any protest over the affair. An alternative, if they want to contribute, is to let them pay for a particular part of your ceremony or reception. For example, they could pay for the band that you thought you couldn't afford, or the menu items that just seemed out of your reach. It can give them a good feeling to know that they are helping, and it can give you and your partner a pleasant surprise at the same time.

Make sure you talk this all over with your partner, because you don't want to get caught up in any family politics with all of the other details you have to worry about. While you're trying to decide, keep in mind that the average, traditional American wedding cost more than seventeen thousand dollars this past year. That was for a very large wedding venue, so if you can knock down that guest list a little, think of how much you can save!

So review your budget and, to the best of your abilities, figure out where you need to make some creative cuts and determine what you can realistically spend. There are ways to save up for the wedding, or to take out a loan if you need to. We just think it's much more creative and fun to think of ways to do this celebration in a way that doesn't make you go into debt over the whole damn thing.

But above all else, remember these six words as you do this: *You don't need to impress anybody!* You've learned that along the way as you've grown to understand who you both really are. Do this for the love of each other, and because the people you are inviting mean a great deal to you. No matter how the ceremony and reception turn out for the two of you, if you do it for these reasons, you'll have managed to make the perfect wedding!

Wedding Attendants

Your Support Team

"I suppose only heaven knows what the secret of love really is.

But even though it may be a secret, it's a secret that

Sandy and I are both sharing together."

SUE

You know that the two of you will be showing up for the wedding and will be standing up front together during the ceremony. Now the question is . . . who else do you want standing up there alongside of you? If we were talking about traditional weddings it would be one or all of the following: the best man, the maid of honor, the groomsmen, and the bridesmaids.

Now, let's get real. One of the fun parts of doing a gay wedding is that you are allowed to think outside the box and beyond tradition. We keep saying that over and over, but we really want to drive home the idea that this ceremony is about the two of you, that it's yours and yours alone. You don't have to follow time-honored but boring traditions that straight society has imposed on heterosexual couples since God knows when. Do you know how many brides and grooms through the centuries wished they could have done what you're now able to do? You're bucking the system!

With that in mind, there is at least one good reason why you may want to at least consider following tradition by having some attendants up there with you during the ceremony. That reason is because they bring with them a most incredible gift: helping hands. Wedding attendants are automatically required by tradition (don't tell them that they don't have to follow it) to help the two of you organize and to "attend" to you (I love that phrase!) before, during, and after the ceremony. That's, obviously . . . duh . . . why they're called attendants.

One of those old stale rules (but possibly handy in this situation) is that most wedding planners will tell you that for every forty guests or so you should have at least two attendants.

Let's take the two best-known attendants, the best man and maid of honor, as an example. To give you an idea of what we're talking about here, we'll list some of the duties that they are traditionally "required" to do. (Tell us, after reading this list, that you can't start to see some damn good reasons to at least consider having them.)

A best man (or woman for that matter):

- Lends moral support to the couple and helps one or both partners as their advisor and personal aide (that's a good enough reason right there!).

- Makes the first toast at the reception.

- Holds (*and does not lose!*) one or both of the partners' rings before the ceremony.

- Oversees the other attendants, working in conjunction with the maid (or man) of honor.

- Witnesses and signs the marriage papers (in those places that recognize our marriages).

- Attends the rehearsal dinner (if the partners are following this tradition) and makes sure everything runs smoothly.

- Throws a "partnership party" before the ceremony, with the couple's prior permission.

- Pays the officiant after the ceremony.

- Dances with both of the partners at the reception.

- Arranges the car for the wedding couple after the ceremony and reception.

- Is responsible for the car's decoration (tastefully, one hopes!).

- Acts as the couple's valet and personal psychiatrist to get them through this whole thing (Wow!).

Now, if you're thinking how valuable it might be to have a friend like that around, wait until you read what some of the duties are for the maid, matron, or man of honor. These two people could become highly invaluable to you, so read the list and really think very strongly before you discard the idea of the possibility of having these two attendants.

The maid, matron, or man of honor:

- Oversees getting all of the dresses and all the fittings and helps to choose the appropriate jewelry to wear (obviously it's important that they have fabulous taste!).

- Helps the couple make up the invitations and oversees the mailing and responses that come in (obviously they'd better have incredible organizational skills, too).

- Keeps a record of all of the gifts given to the couple and secures them in a safe place (hopefully they're honest and won't run off with your toaster!).

- Makes certain that everyone attends the rehearsal who needs to be there.

- Helps to make lodging and transportation arrangements when needed.

- Makes certain that the couple looks beautiful at the ceremony and reception (pointing out any spinach caught between their teeth).

- Oversees the flowers for the wedding party.

- Pounds it into everyone's head that they must arrive early to the ceremony.

- Acts as the glue that holds it all together, with energy to spare, and an infectious laugh for support.

- Holds one or both of the partners' rings during the ceremony, and also doesn't lose them.

- Helps to direct guests during the reception and makes sure they sign the guest book.

- Toasts the couple after the best man's (or woman's) toast.

- Oversees any crises that may arise (must be a great listener and possess a warm heart).

- Helps the couple get dressed before the ceremony and get organized as they leave.

- Acts, at times, as the secretary, candle lighter, style overseer, and the couple's second set of eyes.

- Is someone the couple trusts completely and can turn to at any given moment for moral and practical support, especially when they need it most (wow, this is an incredible person, no?).

A few things to keep in mind when you're deciding who to ask and how many attendants to have: Family and friends can do other jobs if you don't need them to be attendants, including ushering, giving out programs, doing readings, and overseeing requests from either of you. If you have people who want to be helpful, here's your opportunity to spread around the responsibilities and lighten your load (which, trust us, will make you feel a whole lot better in the long run).

Family members can make good attendants, but ultimately it's your choice who you want up there with you. Remember not to allow yourself to be drawn into conflict; everyone should try to be adult enough to respect the decisions that you ultimately make. After all, it's your wedding!

There's no hard and fast rule about the number of males and females in a wedding party, especially when you think outside of that square box. Go with what feels right to you; the rest will work itself out. Remember that four minds—or more—trying to solve a problem can be a heck of a lot better than two.

Whatever combination of attendants you have for your wedding, remember to respect and appreciate the team that you're assembling . . . and thank them at every opportunity you're able to. Everyone needs to feel appreciated, and the ones who care about you the most, and who are helping you out the most, are no exception. Appreciate all of their help and show that appreciation whenever you can.

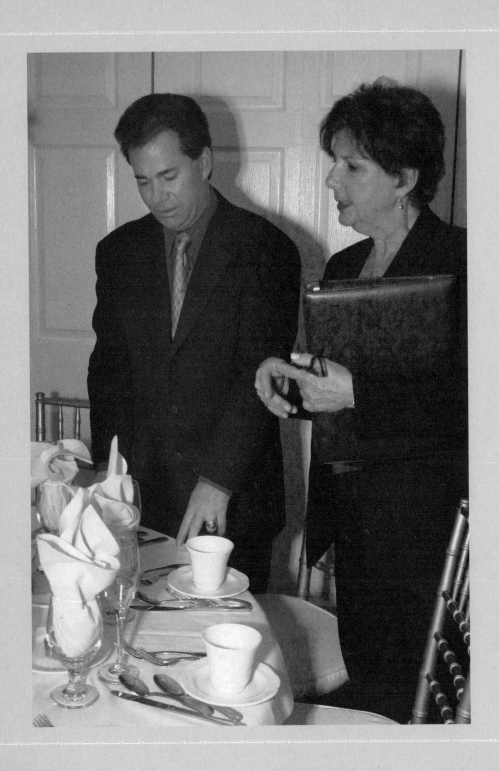

The Wedding Planner

———————

"I learned early on that if I wanted to be happy I needed

something to do. I needed something also that gave me hope.

Most of all, I decided that I needed someone to love.

I found it with Dana . . . that's honestly said. I found

someone to spend my life with."

MICHELLE

One of the most important things for both of you to consider, especially if you live full and active lives, is whether or not to hire a consultant, if you are able to afford it, to take care of all of the wedding details. A consultant can be hired either on a part-time or full-time basis, depending upon your and your partner's needs.

A good source for wedding consultants across the country is our sister site, GayWeddingPlanners.com, or through the Association of

Bridal Consultants, which is a national organization. Just be sure to ask any potential wedding planner whether or not they've done a gay wedding before. Make sure that they're comfortable with the whole concept long before your big day. We've found that most wedding planners have been very friendly and helpful when we needed their guidance.

Wedding planners can help in every phase of preparation and oversee your whole affair, from beginning to end. Most have been trained well to listen to what it is their clients are looking for and are able to put together the couple's dream based on the given budget. They'll do all of the running-around work for you (very important!), and sometimes, through the valuable resources they've built up, can actually save you some money in the long run. It's hard to believe, but when you figure the value of your and your partner's time and the savings through their wholesale contacts, the savings to you can add up very quickly.

You can usually expect to pay them around twelve percent or a little more of the wedding budget, which is certainly not bad when you consider all of the work involved, especially if you're planning on a larger celebration. If they end up saving you money on florists and other vendors, they can almost end up paying for themselves. Most people don't realize this and miss out on a golden opportunity that could have made their life a heck of a lot simpler!

Keep in mind that it has probably taken most wedding planners years to build up the resources that you will spend hours and days looking for—just one more good reason to consider their services. It's very important that both you and your partner make sure that your consultant's personality is in synch with yours, that they give you references you can call, and that they listen closely to what you're looking to have in your ceremony and reception. It is especially important that you be certain to look in their wedding books for the weddings that they've done in the past. Remember that this will be a reflection of their knowledge and, obviously, their taste, and will show you how much these things coincide with yours.

If you want to at least look into hiring a wedding consultant, here is a list of questions you might want to ask.

Questions for Wedding Planners

+ How long have they been in the business?

+ Do they cover everything from A to Z, including being at the ceremony site beforehand, and staying on through the reception?

+ How do they work their commission/pricing?

+ Do they have good contacts for caterers, locations, music, florists, photographers, etc.?

+ Can they work within your budget?

+ Will they be able to get discounts with major vendors? What you would be paying?

+ Do they oversee contracts and negotiations in your best interest?

+ Do they set up timetables and schedules for all those connected with the event?

+ What methods do they employ to keep everyone on schedule?

+ Will the consultant handle all deliveries and setups?

+ Will they help you with wardrobe choices, color schemes, fittings?

+ Will they help do the invitations and mailing, and handle RSVPs?

+ Will they act as troubleshooter, overseeing all aspects of the event?

+ What other duties do they perform that could help make this much easier for you?

As much as you will be interviewing them, they will be trying to learn whether or not you're a client that they will be able to help, and whether they'll be able to share your vision clearly.

If the three of you mix well together, and you find your consultant warm, personable, and responsible, with a steadfast determination, you may very well have met a new friend who can help relieve all of your anxieties in one swift motion of a pen: the signing of the contract.

Dealing with Stress

"Love doesn't keep track of how many wrongs you've put on it.
It's always trusting, hoping, and steadfast. That's what my
lover/partner is to me. She's always there, no
matter where I am."

JACKIE

I have a policy at our inn in Bucks County. It doesn't matter whether the couple getting married is gay or straight. On the night of the wedding, only they are allowed to book a room at the inn. The rest of their family, friends, and guests have to find their own accommodations nearby, and can't stay at the inn with the wedding couple.

Why? Because when you have to deal with family and friends (especially on or around big occasions), there will always be a certain amount of stress involved. It comes naturally from the mix of person-alities. The last thing a newly married couple needs on their first night together as bride and bride, groom and groom, or even, for that matter, bride and groom, is to not have a place they can get away to by them-selves.

All of the factors it takes to plan a wedding can be very stressful. The day (and night) of the wedding should not be. There are tricks we've learned along the way to help our couples relax before the cere-mony. First off, I recommend that they have one of our champagne cocktails, if they drink. Just one, though. The eighteenth-century recipe comes from Doc's family (see "Recipes"). It's wonderful, goes down very smoothly, and helps to mellow anyone who has the pleasure of drinking it.

Now, don't misunderstand me here. The last thing you want to do is to get toasted the hour before you get married. Trust me, with every-thing going on, you don't want your partner second-guessing whether or not you're a lush at the altar, or for them to find you passed out in the bathroom beforehand. That might happen at the reception, but shouldn't happen before!

Anyway, I recommend the *one* champagne cocktail. Also, I always try to get each of them to schedule a massage two hours before the cer-emony. If you're having a big wedding, you'll have your support team to take care of all those last-minute details while you're working at getting yourself relaxed and looking beautiful. In my humble opinion, that's all you should be doing the two or three hours before that ceremony.

If you've elected to have your wedding in a wilderness setting where a massage just isn't practical, take a walk if you can. Clear your head. Look at the beauty around you. Have a friend rub your shoulders and reinforce your self-esteem by telling you how special and beauti-ful you are.

Those few hours before the ceremony are crucial for you. It is your time to be spent thinking about all the good things in your life and how lucky you are just to be you. It's also time to be grateful to a higher power for sending this special someone into your life.

Try to find some quiet time away from the group and relax, maybe curl up in a comfortable chair, even if it's just for ten minutes. Center yourself in whatever ways you know how so that you can be the best you can be as you prepare to go to the ceremony site. Place your cares and worries in your support team's hands. If it's just the two of you having a simple ceremony, do yourself a favor and take a hot bath beforehand and pamper yourself.

During the planning of the wedding, relieve your stress by finding others who can help you to delegate your detail list. You'll be surprised, if you put a little trust in them, how much others are willing to help and how much easier it makes your planning go.

By writing out your priorities and appointing others to help with the tasks, you can focus on the most important aspects of your wedding day and not overly stress yourself. Give your friends or family a chance to help. You'll be relieving your stress and helping yourself to maintain your focus.

If stress and strain come between the two of you, don't let it escalate. Chances are that one of you is not listening to what the other is saying. There is a solution and it doesn't lie in making anything more stressful by blowing it out of proportion. Agree to disagree and look for the common ground. It's there. The answer might not come immediately, but trust me: It will work itself out if you both keep in mind the thing that you are trying to achieve here.

If you find that your temper rises quickly and you're becoming short with each other as you try to navigate through some difficult things in planning, remember that this is a celebration of the two of you. As any of these conflicts arise, be careful not to lash out or blame one another. You're supposed to be celebrating your relationship, not torturing yourselves. Try to handle things as they arise with as much calmness as you can and as much sensitivity as you can each muster.

Find out what each is most interested in doing and what details could be divided between the two of you. And be encouraging to one another. Who knows, that encouragement may end up as a way of life for the both of you. This is a good chance to start practicing it as soon as you both can.

When two partners, no matter how strong the relationship, have to start spending large sums of money (especially when they have to be careful and stick to their budget), it can cause some major stress. That's almost a given. Work it out together as partners, not as business adversaries. Listen to and respect one another's point of view. You are laying the groundwork here for other times in your marriage when there will be a lot of pressure and a lot to be accomplished. Try to sum up each of your points of view as clearly and concisely as you both possibly can. Try to not do it sarcastically, like a short-order cook slinging hash onto the plates.

Ideally the decision-making process in a wedding is equally shared, but many times one partner will tend to carry more of the workload because of circumstances of time or energy. Make sure that if you're the partner who is less involved, you let your partner know how much they're appreciated. Appreciation goes a hell of a long way in times like this. Maybe you could even take your partner out to dinner or a movie or something they would enjoy just to get them away from it all when things pile up. Be clear and explain your purpose. Let them know you care and that you're there. It could mean a great deal at just the right time!

Look over your priorities as they come up. Agree together on the best course of action. Two heads are always better than one. Rate the importance of those priorities and compromise when you have to.

If you disagree on an issue and things get heated, take time to cool off! We can't stress this enough. Wise decisions are rarely made in high-stress/high-anxiety situations with anger flaring in the background. Wait to discuss the issue until you're both more calm. Everything inside of you will want to revolt against that, because you feel that you absolutely need your point of view heard. The problem is, your point of view won't be heard if it's being screamed at the person you care about most in this world. Their defenses will be up on high. Take a breath . . . take a breather . . . and maybe find a way to laugh together, or have a damn cocktail if you both need to!

Be supportive, even when you disagree. Acknowledge your partner's point of view, and remember that the added stress isn't helping to get anything done, just hindering it. It really just becomes energy lost.

Finding a Solution Without Stressing Out: A Personal Story

Two wonderful friends of mine, Ginny and Souby, helped me to work out a stressful situation at a luncheon date I had set up with them.

Before we started eating I told them that time was running out. I told them that I was driving myself crazy over the possible reception menu (I tend to be totally anal-retentive about food), and that I had to find a solution really fast. I was honest with them both and told them that I desperately needed their help or I would end up getting totally overwhelmed.

We had a couple of cocktails and decided—after a lot of laughter—that the best solution was to start out by choosing two different foods that both Doc and I hated: cauliflower and red beets. We laughed about what Doc's expression would be when the plate was set in front of him! I felt the same way.

This little exercise in laughter helped me to calm down and realize that a compromise was closer than I thought. It ended up being a fun and yet productive lunch, all because we started out with laughter and jokes and ended up with solutions by the end of the afternoon!

Remember: *Don't take yourself too seriously* and *don't try to do too much all at once.* Rely on the friends and family you trust to help you relieve your workload of details. The day of the wedding you need to be at your very best, for yourself and for your partner. Relax and take some special time for yourself when you need it.

Remember: Never make the wedding planning more important than the two of you.

Call "time outs" when you need to. If you feel overwhelmed, find a getaway place where you can let it all go for just a while. And very importantly for both of you, don't start throwing blame around on each other. Otherwise you're going to end up with dramas that neither of you need right now. Believe that there is a solution and that even if you don't have it right this minute, it will come if you give it a little time. Try to listen to each other's wants and needs, and both commit to fulfilling them.

Getting It All Together

Being in a committed relationship means that you have to allow for give and take. You're both going to need balance and patience as you try to figure out, "How the hell can we do all of this?"

You may want a lavish blowout reception with a Judy Garland impersonator singing her heart out as you and your beloved dance wildly in front of five hundred plus guests; your partner, on the other hand, wants an informal civil union, performed by a rabbi, with only four of your closest friends and a candlelit dinner in a small private room at an inn: "Maybe a small cake, but absolutely no same-sex cake topper!" If you want to get to that altar and you have these kinds of things going on you'd better learn and understand very quickly what "compromise" means.

Although it can be a very hard lesson to learn at first, the art of compromise will serve you well and make for a long and happy life together if you just learn how it works. The rule of thumb is to find common ground on which you can both agree, and to work from there. If you know your partner wants to keep this private and low key, then respect their wishes if you can live with it. If you're sure they would be happy having a little surprise by finding you've invited ten close, supportive friends to your intimate affair then consider this.

But exercise caution. If your partner is nervous enough as it is over this whole thing, the last thing they need are surprises. Remember, these special times are for both of you, and you should both be making these decisions whenever it is possible. Start by making a checklist of those things on which you both agree, and remember that word: "compromise"!

With that little introduction, and the word "compromise," in mind, let's now get started on the actual creation of the not-totally-perfect-but-still-most-special day of your life.

Creating Your Wedding Style

"I know this sounds so corny, but believe me when I say that it comes from the very center of who I am. Every day I hunger more for the love that shines in her eyes just for me."

MARILYN

Before we start talking about the particular styles you might choose for your wedding, and whether your wedding should be on an intimate or grand scale, formal or informal, let's first talk about the *essence* of any wedding. That essence is romance, and every wedding, no matter the size, should contain elements that lend a romantic nature to the whole affair.

It's important that you keep in mind that you will be basically creating a set design, almost like those in Broadway productions. Even if it is a simple set design (say, for instance, beside a lake) there are certain elements such as lights, flowers, and music that are essential to help create the "magic."

We don't want to make this complicated for you—we know that you probably already have enough on your mind—but you should consider a few things as you begin to design your "set." If neither of you is sure about what might work best, why don't you consider asking those closest to you whose judgment you trust for their ideas? As we said before, if you feel totally stuck already, maybe it's time to consider hiring a wedding planner, especially if you're going for a larger affair. You can also hire one even for only a few hours of consultation. Their advice and professional services can be invaluable if you've reached a point where you're completely saturated and overwhelmed by the possibilities.

With that said, let's consider some of the ideas to keep in mind for that "set design."

The first thing to do is for the two of you to take out a piece of paper and at the top of it put the heading "Romance/Romantic." Ask each other what comes to mind for each of you when you think about these two words. Just write down the ideas or words as they come to you. Use all of your senses. What do you see, smell, taste, hear? When you both think of romance, you will be touching on what the essence of your wedding should be.

Do you see a mountain lake, or a beautiful room with flowing lace, flowers, and rose petals all over the floor? Is it candlelit? What do you hear? What romantic songs are playing in the background? What are you wearing? What tastes can you conjure up in your mind? Continue to ask yourselves these kinds of questions.

Let your imagination take a little flight of fancy here. It's very important for you to do this because it's this imagination that will help you both set the mood and create the look of your set. Do you see candles hanging from the garden trees with a classical guitarist in the background? Or is your style totally different—glitzier and grander, headed off in other directions? What type of place do you both see? A garden, or a beach, or a forest or lake, a quaint country inn, a ballroom, or a charming hotel in Charleston? Are you thinking of mountains, vineyards, or maybe even swaying palms? Don't start to worry that you may have to relocate your wedding to create this dream you're fantasizing about. Realize that by visualizing these places you are providing yourselves inspiration that you can use—on perhaps a smaller scale—to create your ceremony and reception in the style that appeals to both of you.

Think about the flowers that you both like. See them with candlelight. How do they look to you? Flowers and arrangements are very important because they hold some of the most essential qualities for romance . . . almost as essential as candlelight. Let your imagination go further. What kind of lighting do you see? Do you see strings of soft white lights or lanterns hanging all around you? Find the place where both of you converge in your perceptions. Think about the tables and what makes the centerpieces romantic to you—sparkling silver and fine china and glassware? Or do you see beach blankets and picnic baskets? Be honest with one another.

You see, there are so many things to choose from, but the recipe for a successful wedding comes from who the two of you are, and what you need to express your togetherness on your special day. It is all there inside both of you, and this visualization is the beginning of expressing who you both are and what you both want to achieve. If you can find some common ground as to what romance means to both of you, you will be well on your way to knowing what style it is you want to create.

After you do this visualization, there are a few initial decisions you need to make:

+ Domestic partnership, civil union, or state marriage (where allowed)?

+ What will your wedding style be? (Decide on the most important elements that you can agree upon.)

+ Are you going to do a religious ceremony?

+ Indoors or outdoors?

- What time of day—an afternoon or an evening wedding?

- Will the ceremony and reception be an intimate affair or a grand one? (Keep in mind your budget.)

You have to make these choices at the very beginning, because all of these elements will determine the direction of your planning process. These are choices that both of you need to agree upon and be very clear about before you start putting down deposits with vendors and setting up appointments with those who will be contractually involved.

Express Yourself

We encourage self-expression when planning your special day. When trying to work out the details of your ceremony and reception keep in mind that every form of self-expression may not be appropriate or work with your overall plan.

Having been to a wedding or two where things weren't thoroughly thought out, we would like to suggest one thing you might consider *not* doing. If you happen to have a voice that belongs only in the shower with the door closed behind you, please think long and hard before you decide it's absolutely necessary to sing to your partner in front of all your guests! Your partner and the guests attending would greatly appreciate your thoughtfulness in this regard!

Another way for the two of you to start to weave your personalities into your ceremony is by incorporating your heritage. Whether you're African American, Jewish, Italian, Spanish, or from whatever other background, consider finding ceremonial elements that can be incorporated into your planning.

Let's say one of you is of Italian descent. Consider adding an incredible aria from one of your favorite operas as one of your short musical interludes. The concept could be carried over into the reception theme, too: You could even consider adding something like pasta Bolognese as a course instead of a traditional appetizer. There are a hundred tasteful, authentic ways to incorporate your Italian heritage without going too overboard in the process. (Oven-baked pizzas anyone? Don't rule them out for an informal affair!)

This concept can be applied to whatever your two heritages are. Check out the chapter on wedding customs and traditions to get inspiration from different religious and cultural wedding traditions. You could even choose a mixture of cultural traditions for your wedding, from Celtic to Japanese. You don't have to be of a particular ethnic background to appreciate and love the style of it all. Remember, there are no absolutes you have to follow, just as long as you keep your guests in mind (sushi for everyone? *Sayonara!*). The only suggestion we can make is to try to show some good manners, a bit of taste, and a reflection of yourselves—who you really are—into your celebration.

Another popular trend is themed weddings. Any kind of theme that you both agree upon can be used in your wedding ceremony or reception. From Mexican to particular color schemes, from country western to historical . . . the choices are endless. *Olé!*

We've compiled a list of themes from our experiences and a couple that we've heard of from wedding planners. Use this list to spark your imaginations. And if all else fails, you can always do traditional. It's worked for a lot of our gay brothers and sisters already.

Beach Party	Disco	We Are Family
Fiesta	Disney	Camping and Outdoors
Fantasy	Renaissance	Wildlife
Seasonal	Shakespearean	Broadway
Hollywood	Scottish Kilt	Costume Ball
Mardi Gras	Top Hat and White Tie	At The Movies
Viva Las Vegas		Or build a theme around any Culture or Cuisine

And lest we forget . . .

Construction	Leather	Biker

Your Wedding Checklist

"I think we can conquer everything in this world but love. It always ends up conquering us. It didn't matter whether I was beggar, a king, or even a Wall Street jock who thought he knew it all!"

ROBERT

Most wedding books will put all of the things you need to do in a time frame, usually starting one year before the wedding. We've done a wedding before with four weeks' notice! It was crazy, but it worked out fine. It was a smaller wedding, about sixty people, but anything's possible depending on the availability of the location, how fast you can get the invitations out, the support team you have to help you (that's why those wedding attendants are crucial), and the complexity of the affair you're trying to put together.

Jim and Tom had a great team to help them, and most of all they were organized. No one could believe that they could put the whole thing together in that short a time, but it was important to Tom to have the wedding in the U.S., and Jim was being reassigned to Paris for a three-year stint with his job at the last minute. Lucky man!

The wedding and reception was one of the greatest ones I've ever attended. And it wasn't rushed! By the time they made it to the altar, after a whirlwind of work to put the thing together, there wasn't a dry eye in the place when they said their personally written vows to each other.

There was one minor hitch: Someone forgot to pick up their cake and the bakery had closed. We ended up putting together all the desserts that we had at the inn's restaurant into a grand presentation at the last minute. We have great desserts made by Chef Harry, so everyone was happy. The centerpiece of the presentation was chocolate éclairs piled high into what looked like a tower, with vanilla ice cream balls at the bottom. Jim remarked that it was the largest éclair he'd ever seen. Obviously the staff in the kitchen had some fun with it along the way, too!

Jim and Tom were forced to make it happen in a short time—they simply had no choice. Still, they could never have done it without the checklist (see page 70) to keep them on track. The two of you will probably have much more time than they did, so don't worry about it if others think it's impossible to do in just a month. Just make sure you follow your list as you go. Get your friends and family to help when you can, and don't get overwhelmed. When you do, remember to read our chapter about dealing with stress. It helps!

It's important to keep in mind that everything on here is optional (especially if you've decided to throw an informal backyard BBQ after a simple ceremony). Just pick and choose what is necessary for you and cross off the rest. Break it down into easier steps if you need to, but don't put anything off longer than absolutely necessary. This is not rocket science, it's mainly organization and determination. Take it one step at a time, and make sure you're both agreed on those steps. You can do this!

A Few Ideas

Before you get started . . .

Remember to carve out some wedding-planning time when the two of you can get together to have discussions and go over the latest portion of the project. Do this even if just one of you is doing the planning so that you both know you are in synch. You want to make sure your partner is happy with where things are headed, right?

Don't make your whole life revolve solely around the planning. Take occasional "time outs," especially when you feel that stress level rising. Most couples, in the beginning stages, have planning time together usually once or twice a week for an hour or two. Try to hold the planning meeting in a relaxing atmosphere and don't spend the time being negative—that's never very productive.

Be very careful about procrastination, and don't let your Things To Do list get too long. This is one of the greatest causes of stress. Break your planning down into easily reachable goals and keep working at them until they get accomplished.

Share your Things To Do with your attendants or others that have volunteered to help. Spread the work around, don't let it fall just on your shoulders. Make sure your helpers all understand how important it is that they keep you abreast of where they're at and whether or not everything is being accomplished as you want it to be. Have them report to you everything that they've done in great detail so you don't have unwanted surprises later on. Make them feel like they're making an important contribution, because they are!

Keep your emotions in check, as best you can. Don't lose your temper over trivial matters. More importantly, try not to lose your temper in front of others, especially your partner. Even though there may seem to be thousands of details to be taken care of, it's not worth yelling and screaming and making yourself look bad. Take a short break, find your balance, and come back to the task when you feel you can. Apply the principle of breaking things down into manageable tasks and finding a solution.

Follow the checklist as best you can. It's easier to finish each thing and then move on to the next.

Keep a separate journal in your wedding briefcase with all the information needed to complete any particular step. Make sure you do not check anything off until all the details of that part have been finalized.

With all that said, here's your . . .

Wedding Checklist Worksheet

Phase I

- ☐ Set Wedding/Reception Date

- ☐ Announce Your Engagement

    Tell those you care about the most first. (And yes, this usually includes your parents!)

- ☐ Choose Style of Wedding

    - ☐ Formal

    - ☐ Intimate

    Size of Wedding (approximate number of guests)

- ☐ Begin Guest List (in notebook)

    Number after Preliminary Count

- ☐ 10-60 guests

- ☐ 60+ guests

- ☐ Contact Clergy or Officiant; lock in date and time

    Wedding Location

❑ Confirmed

(Call to confirm dates are open, choose another if you need to, or change
original date)

Reception Location (if different)

❑ Confirm

Time of Day

❑ Choose attendants for the wedding party

❑ Each attendant has been called and confirmed

Final list of Attendants and their roles:

❑ Order wedding rings

❑ Pickup date

❑ Complete Gift Registry (if you both agree to do this)

❑ Discuss with your partner possible honeymoons or getaways

❑ Finalize honeymoon plans

❑ Passports in order (if applicable)

❑ Begin to compile song list of favorite songs

❑ Select and order personal stationary and invitations

❑ Pickup date

❑ Set your preliminary budget (see related chapter) $

❑ Choose colors for your affair (see chapter on color)

❑ Primary Color

❑ Secondary Color(s)

❑ Address and mail invitations and RSVPs

❑ Place any public announcement in newspaper (if you both agree)

Phase II

- ☐ Finalize decision on what you and your partner will wear

- ☐ Discuss ceremony and possible readings (see "The Ceremony")

    All readings and readers finalized

- ☐ Reserve lodging for out-of-town guests

    All lodging confirmed and set

- ☐ Set up fitting for you and your partner's outfits; ordered the attire

    Finalize your attire, including all accessories

- ☐ Set up appointments for attendants to be fitted and order attire

    Finalize all attendant fittings

- ☐ Begin to compile a separate list of rental equipment for the ceremony and reception.

Call the rental company to reserve your date, to give a preliminary overview of what you might need, and to reserve your date. Remember that your purpose right now is to just give them an overview of what you might need; you will finalize all of this as you go along.

Note: Your rentals will all be based on your guest count and location. Rentals could include chairs, table covers, china and silverware, glassware, bar supplies, etc. A lot of this will depend upon your event location and what is or is not included with the property. The relationship you establish with the rental company is very important if you plan to host the event yourself, if the location doesn't supply most of these items, or if you do not use the services of a wedding planner.

- ☐ Finalize all rentals necessary for ceremony and reception

- ☐ Set up appointment with a reputable florist to discuss preliminary options for your table centerprieces, floral displays, boutonnières, corsages, etc. (see "Flowers and Florists")

- ☐ Finalize all floral arrangements

- ☐ Set up appointment with the caterer to discuss preliminary menus, wines, etc., if your location does not supply food. (See ✦✦ "Catering Your Affair")

  Finalize all catering arrangements; locked in date

- ☐ Set up appointment with photographer to discuss rates and set date (See related chapter)

  Finalize date/time/type of photos, etc.

- ☐ Make preliminary arrangements for rehearsal dinner (if the two of you agree to have one)

  Rehearsal dinner arrangements finalized

- ☐ Set up appointment with baker for wedding cake

  Finalize choice of cake and cake top

- ☐ All ceremony details completed, including ushers, aisle runner, etc. (See Ceremony Chapter)

- ☐ All reception details completed

- ☐ Order any necessary accessory items like ring pillow, candles, ice sculptures, etc.

- ☐ Decide what type of music you would like at your ceremony and reception. (See "Music, Bands, and DJs")

From there:

- ☐ Meet and finalize musicians to use for ceremony and reception

- ☐ Gave finalized song list

- ☐ Lock in date and time

Phase III

- ☐ Discuss with your partner and attendants arrangements for transportation

  Finalize all arrangements for cars to and from ceremony and reception

- ☐ Finalize all menus and specifics with caterer

- ☐ Finalize all floral arrangements

- ☐ Reconfirm guest count after any last-minute phone calls

  Final Guest Count

- ☐ Begin record book of all gifts that start to come in

- ☐ Purchase small, unique gifts for your attendants

- ☐ Schedule any necessary hair or beauty appointments (This is where you can give your partner the gift of a massage)

- ☐ Buy guest book for everyone to sign

- ☐ Buy and fill out place cards for tables

- ☐ Make the seating arrangements for your guests

Phase IV

(At least three days before the wedding)

- ☐ Check all of your fittings and your attendant's fittings

- ☐ Double-check all professional arrangements, including florist, caterer, music, cars

- ☐ Double-check your wedding checklist. Has everything been checked off?

- ☐ Pack for honeymoon

- ☐ Pick up rings

- ☐ Pre-wedding photos . . . Inform photographer and attendants that shoot will start two hours before ceremony.

Phase V

(Day before wedding)

The full wedding party, readers, officiant, and requested family will attend the rehearsal. Make sure all necessary accessories like candles, runners, etc. are in place. (You may give your gifts to the attendants then or at the dinner afterward if you have chosen to have one.) Be sure that your maid/matron (or man) of honor meets the officiant and the property manager in case they have problems or questions. Give your wedding rings to your two main attendants. Also give them the officiant's envelope, which is to be given to them after the ceremony.

You've arrived!
Congratulations!

PS: Don't forget to send out those thank-yous when you get home from that wonderful honeymoon!

JAMES REGINALD GOLDEN

&

PHILLIP ALAN SAPERIA

INVITE YOU TO SHARE
N THE JOY OF OUR WEDDING AND THE
BRATION OF OUR THIRTY YEARS TOGETHE
NDAY, THE THIRTY FIRST OF OCTOBER,
TWO THOUSAND AND FOUR
CHESHVAN SIXTEEN,
HOUSAND SEVEN HUNDRED SIXTY FI

Y IS REQUESTED
H OF SEPTEMBER

Your Guest List and Invitations

TINA: *What do I remember about our invitations? You should ask Jennifer about that one.*

JENNIFER: *I worked really hard on those. It took me almost a month to find the right card, and then addressing those things nearly killed me!*

TINA: *Now tell him the rest of it.*

JENNIFER: *(Hesitating) I went to the post office with all of them . . . and got the stamps . . . and it was a hot day . . . so we all went down to the beach . . . and . . . well . . . a couple weeks later, one of our best friends finally asked me why we didn't invite her to the wedding.*

TINA: *She left the invitations in the damn trunk!*

elieve it or not, the best way to make out your wedding guest list is to invite everybody you could possibly want to come. From there, you begin to pare down the list by using a reality check.

Start by throwing out the negative drama queens (unless, of course, one of them is your mother). Next, drop all those people you haven't seen in years; you probably aren't close to them anyway and they don't need an invitation, unless there is a chance they may be leaving you an inheritance! Next, take out the excess folks that you wouldn't be heartbroken not to see there anyway. And keep in mind your reception space—that'll help to get you in the right frame of mind to do this.

Lastly, start to really consider what your budget is going to be. Believe me: That will become a truly motivating factor to bring the guest list down to a reasonable number! This is probably where, if you haven't had the inclination yet to do so, you'll consider bumping all of the kids off the list and make it an adult-only ceremony, except for your own children or those in the wedding party. I can't tell you how many couples who hadn't thought of that idea said to me, "What a great idea. We can blame it all on you!" And proceeded to do so!

If you have to make a choice between distant family or close friends, the choice should be obvious to you. If it isn't, let your partner make the choice, because it's obvious you're already getting way too overwhelmed!

In your decision-making, decide whether you're going to allow either set of your parents to have a say in any guests that should be invited. In most straight weddings they almost always have a say. In yours, with your untraditional thinking, they will probably have very little say in who your guests are, but might still insist on inviting Great Aunt Edna, who you thought had passed on years ago. Let's hope she doesn't decide to pass on when she learns of your choice for a spouse!

— ⁌⁍ —

Your Invitations

There are some ground rules to follow when you're making out your wedding invitations. Make sure all your invites have the names of any significant others added, and that you have all of their names spelled correctly and the addresses are double-checked for accuracy. It's also important to be sure to include maps for those out-of-town guests.

Your biggest source for invitations is often a stationery store, or you can shop online at GayWeddingStore.com. The stationery stores will have enough catalogs to make your eyes water, so don't worry that you won't have enough choices. Private printers usually do engraving if you've decided to get real fancy.

There's now a wide assortment of male/male and female/female cards available, too. One day we hope that the major card companies will even get in on this, but until then, you can either look for them online or have an artist design you something especially for you. Two designs that are very popular right now are the two tuxes on the front (for men) and the two wedding dresses (for women), although we all know that those design choices don't address all the attire options, especially when it comes to our community.

Interwoven initials are another very popular invitation motif right now. Of course they can also echo the colors, flowers, or theme used throughout your wedding design. It all depends on how formal or informal your wedding will be and your individual style and taste.

As to what the printing on the invitation should say, well, this is where you can make your announcement, literally, if you choose to. Most couples begin the invitation with their names and then invite guests to their ceremony:

John Stewart and Paul Cox
cordially invite you to their wedding . . .

Use humor if you want to; just be careful that you don't make your guests nervous about everybody coming in drag or something. (Unless of course you want everybody to be in drag. That we leave entirely up to you!)

As far as the typeface or font to use on the invitation, you'll be amazed at the variety. There are computer programs now that can almost perfectly mimic handwritten calligraphy. Although calligraphy is truly an art form, these reproductions can fool all but the best-trained eye.

You might want to consider, at the same time you're having your invitations designed, having your thank-you cards, your personal stationery, and maybe even some cocktail napkins designed and printed as well. You might get a better price on the job when you do it in bulk like this. That's all up to you.

The rule in ordering is to make up your guest list first so that you know how many invitations you'll need to order. Next, order at least thirty more invitations than you expect to send. (I know this seems like a lot, but especially if you're having a bigger celebration, for the little extra cost it's better to be safe than sorry.)

Decide if you want to include response cards (it's usually done, but hey, we're thinking outside the box here). Guests can RSVP by phone . . . or even send a pigeon if you want—you decide.

According to traditional thinking, you're supposed to always use proper titles, or so the elegant wedding books say: "Mr. and Mrs. _____ ," etc. I find this too traditional for me personally. Most of my hetero women friends don't even care to be addressed as "Mrs." even if they do have their husband's last name. "Sally & Wayne Dylan" works for them and me too. But again, that's solely your choice to make.

If you're hand-addressing the envelopes, use a black pen (preferably) and make sure that people can read your writing (especially the postal clerk). If your writing is really bad, let your partner do it or a wedding attendant. You can even make a group party out of the whole thing. The writing out of invitations can be a hand-breaking job. Consider getting as much help as you can to help the two of you through it. The more the merrier, especially if you're planning a big wedding. Just hold the martinis, cosmos, or beer until after you're done—have a little consideration for that poor damn postal clerk!

Keep in mind that your invitation is the first taste the guests will get of your big day. Even though it's not the biggest detail your guests will remember, it will definitely help to set the tone you are going for. After you have made your guest list and checked it twice (including the correct spelling of names, etc.), then you get your invitations made.

As it is with almost every aspect of weddings, choices abound when it comes to invitations. You could sit and look at twenty-five samples and wrack your brain trying to detect what the actual difference is between them, only to discover that it's only a fraction of a shade from one color to the next.

Then there's the paper stock, font, and size to contend with, and here, too, there are many, many choices. Getting out there and seeing samples is your best bet. There are stationers who do this full time, but nowadays, with more computer-savvy couples, making your own is not a bad idea. It all depends on the quality and look you are shooting for. If you decide to make your own, consider that the paper stock will not be commercial quality, but that's not saying it won't look great.

If you do decide to hire a professional, look at all of their samples and ask to have samples to take with you. If you're ordering online, most places can send you samples in the mail. It's really important for you to actually feel the paper before you commit to it because paper stocks can vary greatly. Important characteristics to keep in mind when ordering or making your invitations are paper stock, font, and size.

After everything is printed, you will have to assemble and address the invitations. These are the components of your invitation: outer and inner envelopes, reception card, response card, and response envelope.

THE OUTER ENVELOPE: This is the envelope that is addressed and stamped and holds everything to follow.

THE INNER ENVELOPE: This envelope has the guests' names on it and holds everything to follow.

THE RECEPTION CARD: This is the who, why, what, and where. This is the card that will tell the guests where to go and at what time. You may also include a map on this card or with it.

THE RESPONSE CARD: This card will have two options: "I will attend" or "I am unable to attend," one of which your guests will choose. Also, meal choices are usually included on the response card. RSVP date should be two to three weeks prior to the wedding. This will give you time to make a seating chart if you'd like.

THE RESPONSE ENVELOPE: This holds the response card and is addressed to go back to you.

The last big thing to remember with your invitations is that they ideally go out eight weeks before your actual date. This gives guests plenty of time to clear their schedules and make travel arrangements if they are coming from out of town.

Choosing a Location

"Well, simply put, she's the one I love. Pure and simple.
This old world just can't help but be a better
place because of that."

LESLIE

Finding the perfect place to have your ceremony can be a daunting task, to say the least. There are a few questions that you need to answer before making your final decision. Begin with setting the date, one that works for you and your partner and one that hopefully won't conflict with your closest friends' and familys' schedules. You will need to do this nine to twelve months in advance, if possible, in order to secure any facility's availability and also to lock in your choice of time.

Finding the perfect ceremony and reception site will be one of the most important components you will have to decide upon for your celebration. This will be the place where all of your wedding memories will take place. It should be somewhere that you both agree on and feel comfortable in.

You will also have to decide whether to have your ceremony and reception indoors or out. Usually the reception takes place indoors or under a tent to protect you from the elements. Tents have to be set up hours in advance and may require heating units. It's a necessity to have backup plans for bad weather to make your affair a success no matter what the weather decides to do. If any part of your ceremony or reception is to take place outdoors, be sure to let your guests know so that they can dress accordingly. (High heels on expansive tracts of lawn can be a pain.)

Remember to also keep in mind the logistics of your two venues. How far of a drive (or walk) is it from the ceremony site to the reception facility? Make it easy, logistically, for yourselves and for your guests. Be creative in the planning, and if you don't feel like walking and it's not too great of a distance, consider getting a horse and carriage (or a Ferrari convertible, for that matter) to take you to your reception. (See our chapter on transportation.)

Many couples choose to have the ceremony and reception in one place. This idea can cut down tremendously on logistical difficulties and can help to save you a great deal of money. Flowers and rentals only have to be set up once when they are both at the same place. For this reason alone it could be a huge savings to you both, and is worth consideration. Another benefit is that your guests won't have to spend a lot of time traveling from one place to another, which gives you much more time to party!

In choosing the site, make it a meaningful location, whether it's the place where you first met, your local home area, or even a destination wedding if your budget allows. Make the choice as a couple, both contributing to the final decision—a decision that will be a matter of your combined style, religious background, and budget, as well as the size of the affair.

Your wedding day will pass quickly and you only have a limited number of hours in which to have everything take place. This is important to remember when you're considering your location and the distances involved. Also keep in mind the logistics of the space that you will be working with. Make sure there is plenty of room to spare for the various activities that will take place. The location you pick and the season of the year will set the whole tone for your celebration.

Be sure to check for location availability dates before you announce your wedding date. Once the location decision is made and locked in you'll have finalized one of the most important aspects to the whole planning process.

If you are planning a destination wedding at some far-off place (which is becoming tremendously popular these days) remember that you are not under any obligation to pay for your guests' flights or hotel rooms.

Although a destination wedding can be an appealing idea, you have to keep in mind the financial burden it may impose on your guests to attend. If you have your heart set on one, call several airlines to see if they offer any group-rate flights or discounted fares. Be sure to contact the hotels where your guests might be staying to ask them the same thing. You'll be finding out availability at the same time and will know what is or isn't possible. Consider booking in the off season to get even better rates.

The Great Outdoors

Indoor venues offer protection against the elements and give us our creature comforts. Some indoor venues have terraces with views or outdoor garden areas with shelter close by in case the weather takes a turn for the worse. But oh . . . when you think of the great outdoors, imagine the possibilities! Birds singing, waves lapping, sun setting, brook babbling, views for all to enjoy! That's nature at its best.

But just to cover all your bases, take some time to consider nature at its less-than-best! Bugs biting, wind blowing, rain falling, temperatures dropping! Always with the good comes the possibility of the bad. Outdoor weddings can provide the most romantic, beautiful settings of all. But if you're planning your wedding outdoors, your primary consideration will have to be what to do just in case of bad weather. Make a backup plan—that's the best advice we can give you. Just in case!

If you select an outdoor location, be sure to have an indoor space nearby if it starts to rain, snow, or if it get too cold or hot. Your goal is to make sure that your guests are comfortable at all times, not baking in the sun, getting poured on, or freezing their collective buns off.

One of the most wonderful things about outdoor weddings is that the decorations can usually be kept to a minimum if you're surrounding yourself with natural beauty. Be sure to visit your site at different times of the day to check out the lighting conditions. Go there a few days beforehand to make sure that everything is looking great and that there isn't grass that needs mowing or flowers or shrubs to be pruned. Be sure to replace any necessary plants or flowers and add color wherever it might be needed.

Depending on your geographic location, summer, autumn, winter, or spring may be hot. Be sure to have a cooler of iced water bottles available. Another option is to provide inexpensive hand-held fans and let your guests fan themselves off during the ceremony if they need to. You can also consider renting some large outdoor fans, or put up that tent to provide some shade.

If it might be damp or cold, consider putting an insert in your invitation reminding guests to dress accordingly. Add portable heaters if you think it might get cold, or even go so far as to have a stack of throws for those who might get uncomfortable easily, especially your older guests.

One of the weather conditions that could arise is a windy day. Plan ahead to make sure everything is battened down beforehand so that you won't be frazzled if a wind should happen to pop up unexpectedly.

Other Tips

- Have large stands filled with umbrellas for your guests.

- Make sure your caterer knows how to plan for a menu that is tailored to outdoor eating (this should include items that hold up well in the heat).

- Consider the insects or bees that might decide to attend your affair along with your guests. Have some citronella candles on the side and even a bottle of "bug bomb."

- Consider the placement of the chairs and altar. Make sure they don't face into the sun so that your guests are blinded and unable to see the two of you up there doing your thing.

- Also think about the time of day for your ceremony; there's nothing like an incredible sunset to make it absolutely perfect, if you can time it right!

- Be sure to include some hydrating liquids like iced tea, lemonade, or iced water. Alcohol can have a very dehydrating effect.

- If you have a tent, be sure that it's anchored well. It's better to be safe than sorry.

- Don't forget to tell your hairstylist that you might have to be sprayed extra to hold your hair in place if there's any possibility of wind.

- If you need to add visuals, consider flower-covered arches or trellises. They're fairly inexpensive but the look goes a long way in adding romance to your ceremony. Also consider the candles you want to use, their placement, and whether or not to use additional lawn torches for effect.

- If you're holding the ceremony in a park, be sure you contact your zoning or parks department for any necessary permits. Ask them about guidelines for alcohol, trash, and outdoor lighting, especially torches or candles.

The Ceremony

"I knew one day I wanted a family, but I didn't know if it would ever be possible. Now I look around at the two kids we have and see so much more love here than I ever grew up with. My dream came true and I couldn't have done it without my partner."

JOAN

Okay. You've decided on a domestic partnership or civil union, you've planned your wedding style and whether or not your ceremony will be religious or secular. Now it's time for you to orchestrate the ceremony itself. Here we'll discuss the components of ceremonies, as well as the pros and cons of various venues and large or more intimate affairs.

Generally, ceremonies will differ depending upon whether you're Protestant, Catholic, Jewish, or a member of another religious group.

Check on our website for gay-friendly clergy who can help you with finding a gay-friendly officiant.

If you have permission to have the ceremony in a church (yes, several churches now do allow this!) ask about lighting of the candles, the approval for flowers and decorations, parking allowance, the time frame for the wedding, receiving lines, and other important questions you've compiled. Find out what's permissible and what isn't, and know ahead of time.

If your ceremony is not to be held in a church, synagogue, or other religious house, you've probably decided to have it at a club, an inn, a beautiful home, or a natural setting of some sort. In any case, be sure to lock in the date and time of your event with the owner of the venue. Also be sure to allow extra time for any necessary setup, breakdown, or cleanup. If your reception follows the ceremony at the same place, you will have a lot less work to do than if it is at separate places.

No matter what type of ceremony you decide upon, whether religious or secular, it can be a truly beautiful moment in time that neither of you will ever forget. When you meet with your gay-friendly officiant, have a list of questions so that you will feel comfortable with the particular procedures involved. Include questions on their fee, suggested readings, and the order of the ceremony.

It's good to remember, as you start to plan your ceremony with its various elements like vows, unity candles, songs, and readings, that no two weddings are ever the same. If done correctly, each will reflect the personalities of the two people who are committing themselves to each other. Lesbian and gay weddings have been known to run the gamut of possibilities because of the uniqueness of the people getting married, from scuba weddings to nude beach weddings (so we hear) to Elvis-officiated weddings held in Las Vegas!

We've found, and middle America may find this hard to believe, that of all the weddings taking place these days in our community, it's the traditional wedding styles that seem to be followed most. The white lace and black tie affairs win hands down. But it's the personalization and uniqueness of who these couples are that adds the extra flair.

The second choice in the community seems to be the (informal or formal) wedding celebration which is held when the couple returns home from one of the states or cities where unions are recognized in one form or another.

On our site GayFriendlyInns.com we list at present over one thousand gay-friendly inns that either allow weddings to be performed or at least welcome gay and lesbian couples from around the country to come and stay with them. It's a great place to start if you're looking for a friendly place to stay and possibly have your ceremony, as many of the inns and businesses we list have been on board with us since long before national advertisers realized the monetary benefits of working with our community. Here are just a few that really stand out:

Arizona

Alma de Sedona Inn, Sedona
www.almadesedona.com

California

Inn at Occidental, Occidental
www.innatoccidental.com

Caliente Tropics Resort, Palm Springs
www.calientetropics.com

Handlery Union Square Hotel,
San Francisco
www.handlery.com

Nob Hill Hotel, San Francisco
www.nobhillhotel.com

Handlery Hotel & Resort, San Diego
www.handlery.com

Colorado

The Denver Marriott South at Park
Meadows, Littleton

www.marriott.com/denms

Delaware

Sea Witch Manor Inn,
Rehoboth Beach

www.seawitchmanor.com

Georgia

Kehoe House, Savannah
www.kehoehouse.com

Hawaii

Hale Kipa 'O Pele, Kailua Kona
www.gaystayhawaii.com

Louisiana

Magnolia Mansion, New Orleans
www.magnoliamansion.com

Massachusetts

The Eliot Hotel, Boston
www.eliothotel.com

Holiday Inn Select Boston Government
Center, Boston
www.bostonholidayinnselect.com

The 1684 Burnham House, Essex
Phone: (978) 768-6356

Inn at West Falmouth, Falmouth
www.innatwestfalmouth.com

Cape Codder Resort & Spa, Hyannis
www.capecodderresort.com

John Carver Inn, Plymouth
www.johncarverinn.com

Carpe Diem, Provincetown
www.carpediemguesthouse.com

The Dan'l Webster Inn, Sandwich Village,
www.danlwebsterinn.com

Broken Hill Manor, Sheffield
www.brokenhillmanor.com

New Jersey

Carroll Villa Victorian Hotel, Cape May
www.carrollvilla.com/rooms

Pillars of Plainfield B&B Inn, Plainfield
www.pillars2.com

New York

RIHGA Royal New York Hotel,
New York
www.rihgaroyalny.com

Hilton Pearl River, Pearl River
www.hiltonpearlriver.com

Oregon

Portland's White House B&B, Portland
www.portlandswhitehouse.com

Tennessee

Prospect Hill B&B Inn,
Mountain City
www.prospect-hill.com

Vermont

The Lilac Inn, Brandon
www.lilacinn.com

The Black Bear Inn, Bolton Valley
www.blkbearinn.com

The Inn at Essex, Essex
www.innatessex.com

Cortina Inn, Killington
www.cortinainn.com

The Castle, Proctorsville
www.thecastle-vt.com

Timberholm Inn, Stowe
www.timberholm.com

The Pitcher Inn, Warren
www.pitcherinn.com

Grunberg Haus, Waterbury
www.grunberghaus.com

Moose Meadow Lodge, Waterbury
www.moosemeadowlodge.com

Your ceremony will start to take shape as you start exploring some of the options outlined in this chapter. To make the planning go more smoothly for both of you, just be yourselves and let your creative juices flow. Remember that your guests will be people you love. Resist the temptation to go overboard just for the sake of doing so. Make it honest and straight from your hearts and you'll end up with not a dry eye in the place! We've seen it many times.

⟷

Writing Personal Vows

The secret to this endearing moment of the ceremony is to keep the vows short, but straight from the heart. If you do it this way, you'll knock 'em dead! And more importantly, you'll touch each other's souls. We have seen it happen time and again at numerous gay and lesbian weddings. (See "Writing Vows" for further suggestions.)

Finding Your True Song

Music will play a very important part in the overall mood and feel of your ceremony. From the beginning music that is played (the Prelude), to your entrance (Processional), to the music during the ceremony (the Interlude), and finally to your exit down the aisle as one shared heart (Recessional), music is the glue that holds it all together. (See "Music, Bands, and DJs" for more.)

All of these important elements, along with the insights from your officiant, will give you the beginnings to build a ceremony that is uniquely based upon the two of you. Put them together, authentically, and you won't have to ask anyone if they were touched in incredible ways.

Intimate vs. Grand Affairs

Do you want a clambake down at the oceanside with a simple ceremony on the beach, or are you thinking tuxes and champagne at an award-winning resort? Most couples usually have an idea about where they want the ceremony and reception to be, and that location will usually dictate whether it will be an informal or formal affair. Be certain that you are making a conscious choice for the two of you. Make your decision and lock it all into place ahead of time.

You can start out with one idea about the size of your guest list and move very quickly to a much larger venue. This usually happens when the wedding invitation list starts to grow out of control. This is great if the two of you have decided this is what you want, just make sure that you have decided it and that things aren't just getting a bit out of control. If it's a case of losing control, it's time to start wittling down that invitation list—quickly! Remember that a much larger venue can be a major strain on your budget and a hell of a lot more work . . . especially if it wasn't something that was planned for.

A Story from the Inn

At one of our recent weddings, the sister of one of the brides held a small pearl "blessing bag" at the entrance to the church. As all of the guests came in she told them that the brides' rings were in the bag, and she asked each person as they passed if they would just hold the bag for a moment and send their blessings to the couple. All of the guests eagerly clutched the bag, sending their good thoughts toward the couple.

Part of the creativity displayed in most gay weddings may come from a reluctance to follow traditional lines because we know that gay or lesbian weddings never have been, and probably never will be, the norm. In other words, no rules! Don't you just love it?

Formal Weddings

A formal wedding is like "putting on the Ritz." It's a combination of romance and sophistication, all done in a first-class presentation. Check out any movie where Cary Grant was headed to any celebration party, especially the wedding scene from *The Philadelphia Story*. That'll give you a feel for the whole thing. And be sure you break out the champagne and caviar!

Whether it's taking place at a yacht club or country club, or some other ritzy venue, you can bet that you'll be seeing your fair share of palm trees, high ceilings, and chandeliers. But you don't need a million bucks to put on one of these affairs. You can come pretty close to the concept even if you are working on a somewhat tight budget.

There are a few key elements that are important to a formal look. Here are just a few tips for you to consider:

+ Rent ballroom chairs, not folding chairs, and be sure to have nice cushions.

+ Make sure your reception space has a large dance floor.

+ Think bigger and grander when it comes to things like tall candelabras and flower arrangements. Make your table centerpieces overflowing and rich-looking by using trailing ivy and boxwood.

+ Consider renting large potted plants, especially palm trees and the like, to fill the space.

+ Don't use streamers or plastic glasses—they kill the mood.

+ The same holds true for drinks: Forget the beer and go for classics like martinis, cosmopolitans, and champagne cocktails with a slice of strawberry in the glass.

+ Use expensive-looking fabrics and large, folded napkins for your tables. You can even buy your fabric at a wholesale place and have it sewn.

+ Add tall candelabras and some floating candles spaced around to add to the feel of elegance.

+ Consider a large ice sculpture, perhaps with moss and orchids strewn around the piece.

+ Consider serving fine wines and be sure to have a champagne cocktail toast to the couple.

+ Rent or acquire the best china you can.

+ The hors d'oeuvres and champagne should always be passed on silver trays.

+ For a formal affair, music is one of your most important key elements; choose wisely so that the two of you set the mood that you want. Buy a few CDs beforehand and learn which combination you like best, whether it's a classic singer like Frank Sinatra or a full orchestra. NOTE: Make sure you know how to dance to the music you choose, because you're going to end up out on that dance floor with just the two of you, even if you don't think you will.

+ Be sure to buy lavish favors for your guests. The trick is to find things that look like they cost a fortune, but in reality didn't. Consider small silver frames with the date of your wedding inside, or cigars for the men (and some of the ladies, too), or as a last resort, some chocolate truffles in a beautiful, small gold or silver box.

A Story from the Inn

I've done many weddings over the years at the inn. The majority of them were formal in look, and I can honestly say that you can have a formal wedding without spending all of the money you have. Be creative and take time to define what it is you're after.

Let me give you a little example of what creativity can do. Two brides who were getting married, both teachers on a budget, wanted to have a luncheon wedding to save on costs, instead of having a large Saturday-night affair. They invited sixty guests so it would be a formal, yet intimate celebration. They selected carefully from the menu and stayed away from the higher-priced items. They included a champagne cocktail toast (a requirement at my inn), and they only had the open bar for one hour, to further cut down on costs. They served wine with their luncheon and had a wonderful classical guitarist who played throughout.

Still, with all their cut corners, they realized that they did not have much left over for flowers, which can be a huge part of the expenditure if you're not careful. They were such a wonderful couple, we all fell in love with them both the minute we met them. You just couldn't help it. I told

* Choose the clothes for the two of you carefully. Remember that elegance and style sometimes come with simplicity. It's the fit and the fabric that will show you have good taste, even if your outfit happens to be leather.

Intimate Weddings

Intimate weddings can be done at many different types of locations, and usually have a much smaller group of people, up to about seventy-five. An intimate wedding could be held at your favorite restaurant or inn (if they have a private room or garden), outdoors at a favorite nearby park (make sure you are allowed and have permission when them not to worry about the flowers, that the inn would give this as a gift to them and that we could do some kind of simple centerpieces that would look nice.

I got up early in the morning, and with two of my staff, went out into the garden. It was June and everything was in bloom. What started out as simple table centerpieces ended up in extravagance. We couldn't stop ourselves and the vases and flower displays were filled with hydrangea, bear grass, roses, ferns, and ivy sweeping all across the tables and gazebo.

When Tina and Gerry came in, the place was alive with color and beauty, and they both had tears in their eyes because of what my staff had done with only the blossoms growing right outside the inn.

The point is, there are creative ways to make your affair look lavish if you want to. Just find ways to make it happen through imaginative ideas. When you're stuck and don't have the answer, ask your support team for suggestions. In Tina and Gerry's case, it was right under our noses. That old saying still holds true: "Where there's a will . . . there's a way!"

necessary), by a family pool, at the beach, or a million other places. Intimate weddings allow for a closer camaraderie between yourselves and your guests.

These weddings can be formal, but usually some of the grand traditions are dropped, such as a larger wedding party, flower girls, or ring bearers. The staging creates a much more personal touch that is reflected in many other ways: the couple is part of the whole celebration, more up close and personal than in a larger affair. In grander, formal affairs, oftentimes there are unfamiliar faces. Not so in the intimate celebration. The guests are the people in the couple's lives and are there to show their loving support and share in their special moment. At a recent intimate wedding, after dinner each guest (there were twelve) made a brief, very personal toast to the couple. It was a warm and moving experience filled with laughter, tears, and lots of champagne! Intimate affairs allow the couple and those close to the couple to truly share the celebration.

Usually the budget is much smaller, but because of the smaller number of guests, there can be more expenditure in the elements that mean the most to you as a couple. Perhaps you want to upgrade your food selections or wine choices, or maybe you'd rather have live music than a DJ. During the planning of an intimate wedding, the couple can feel a greater amount of flexibility to make an unforgettable evening or afternoon for those they really care about.

The freedom to choose your location is also much broader when there are fewer guests and you're not looking for a ballroom-type atmosphere. Intimate affairs can be done almost anywhere, from private clubs to public parks to choice restaurants. It's important though, to keep in mind that even though the wedding is intimate, the details will be noticed even more than at a larger, formal affair. There are no big rooms or crowds of people in which to get lost. Everyone there will play a part in the whole affair. Your tables should be larger (one or two tables of twelve rather than two or four tables of six) and round or oval, creating a more engaging environment.

NOTE: One drawback to be aware of: The hardest part about having an intimate wedding is the moment when the two of you (and your families) realize that you can't invite everyone. Be ready to deal with some hurt feelings among distant family members and casual friends when they can't understand why they're not being invited. One way to deal with this is to either make the reception larger, invite more people to come afterwards, or to have a large party a few weeks later where everyone can come. This can go a long way to smooth any ruffled feathers.

Then of course, there's always the option to have your wedding on a Caribbean island or some other exotic place where only a few could attend anyway.

I know that we keep repeating ourselves, but keep in mind this thought: Your creativity is unlimited when it comes to figuring out what is right for the two of you. It's your day . . . don't forget that!

A Word About Officiants

When you choose someone (whether a clergy member, justice of the peace, or someone else) to perform the nuptials for you and your partner, you are obviously choosing someone who will end up directing and steering the very heart of your ceremony. They should ideally be someone who has many of the same beliefs and ideals that the two of you share in common. An officiant can be instrumental for both of you in the final design of your vows. Hopefully they will be respectful of what your desires are for the ceremony and help you feel at ease.

Your ceremony should be trouble free, and flow smoothly. Try to meet with your officiant a few times to make sure everything is familiar to you beforehand.

The officiant should be able to attend your rehearsal and help direct you and your party using their professional guidance.

Get to know your officiant if you can so that you can feel at home with them. You'll need that reassurance of familiarity when the time comes and you both stand at that altar.

Sign a contract or rent out the church, if they so request, and lock in the date with them before you announce your wedding date.

The officiant should be one of the first people to arrive for the ceremony. Choose someone who has experience and preferably someone who is a gifted speaker.

If this is a religious officiant, check the rules and regulations of their particular organization to make sure you meet any special requirements that they might have. Religious officiants know the protocol for their religious ceremonies and many times have suggestions on things to add to your ceremony that will help to make it more in keeping with your particular ideas.

Don't hesitate to ask questions, especially if either of you is uncertain about any portion of what is being planned. Be comfortable and remember: This is your day. That's what it's all about.

Writing Vows

Finding the right words to say

"What I learned after I met my partner was that without that love of his . . . there ain't never gonna be enough!"

ISAAC, FROM MISSISSIPPI

If there is one way to make your ceremony unique, it's in the act of writing your personal wedding vows. They allow you not only to honestly express the way you feel, but also to express who the two of your are individually and as partners together.

Wedding planners, when asked to help a couple with ideas for vows, sometimes have a questionnaire for each of them to fill out separately. Then the partners usually compare notes together. The questions are usually designed to get both of your minds—and hearts—focused on what moves each of you when you think of the other.

We've outlined one such questionnaire below. It works best if you both find a relaxed place where you can think and let your feelings out on paper, by yourself. It doesn't have to be perfect when you first write the answers, it just has to come from the heart.

Trust me, you will do fine if you just try to be sincere and honest. Don't try to make it overly "sugary," just make it the real way you honestly feel. Answer the questions as openly as you can and everything will work out fine—watch and see. Remember, <u>do this first section separately</u>, not together in the same room. Allow yourselves enough time to finish comfortably without disturbing each other. Make sure you aren't rushed. Try putting on some of your favorite music softly, sit in your favorite chair in a room that you find comfortable, and see if that helps you with the flow of the writing.

In the second part of this exercise, the two of you will compare notes, unless of course you want the vows to be a surprise. However, I highly recommend you consider doing this together, not leaving things up to chance. The bond between you will grow stronger as you put your deepest feelings for each other into words. In addition, you have to keep in mind that at the wedding you're both going to be very nervous.

Practicing the five or six lines that you come up with through this exercise is going to make you more comfortable, and you will know ahead of time that your partner is touched by what you've written.

——◆——

Vow-Writing Exercise

Write as much, or as little, as you feel. (There are some key words you might want to use at the end of this exercise.) This is not a test, it is an expression of your love. You automatically get an A+ just for trying. Do the best you can—that's all anyone can ask.

Think over the wonderful times the two of you have spent together. Take a few minutes to think about those special times.

1. My partner made me laugh so incredibly hard when _____ (*tell the story*).

2. I love my partner because _____.

3. One of the times that my partner touched my heart deeply that I will always remember was _____ (*think of acts of kindness, generosity, or love*).

4. I can describe my partner with the following adjectives: _____ (*use several, from tender to comical. Write any short personal story that comes to mind*).

5. The things that make my partner stand out from the crowd are _____ (*use descriptive words or phrases*).

6. When I realized I was in love, it felt like _____ (*reminisce about the way that the two of you met*).

7. When I think of my partner lovingly I feel _____.

8. Think of any loving nicknames that you call your partner. Write them down.

9. My partner has taught me _____.

10. I think I've taught my partner _____.

11. The special words that come to mind when I think about my partner are: _____.

12. One of our favorite songs is _____.

13. If I were to try to think of any words from a song to describe us together it would be the words _____.

14. Finish answering the following (feel the love in your heart as you do):

    a. My partner inspires me to _____.
    b. The two things I admire most about my partner are _____ and _____.

     c. If my partner were not in my life I would be _____

        because _____.

15. Marriage means the following to me: _____.

16. I want to marry my partner because _____.

Okay, you both did a great job. Praise each other for getting through this! Now take turns reading out loud your answers to each question.

I know this is almost asking too much, but you need to know how the other feels and practice not being embarrassed to do so. This is very important because you will be condensing what you wrote into a few lines after you read to each other.

Once you are finished reading your answers to each other, take the papers you each wrote on and <u>underline any favorite words, phrases, or sentences that stuck out in your minds</u>. Talk about what you've underlined, and then take a fresh piece of paper for each of you.

At the top, put the following words:

I, _____ choose to have you _____ to be my
_____ from this day forward, because _____.

This is to just get the process started for each of you.

Work at the writing, using your key words, sentences, and phrases. Embellish as you wish as you write your vows. (Some partners prefer to do this by themselves and fine-tune it with their other half after they have worked on it for a while. The choice is up to the two of you.)

Be sure to keep fine-tuning your vows over the next few days until you are both comfortable with the words and the meaning you are trying to convey. Practice saying them together, holding hands and looking into each other's eyes. You'll be surprised at how helpful this exercise can be. Try it! We believe you are going to be deeply touched and moved by what you hear from each other.

Key words to use or keep in mind

Honor, respect, cherish, encourage, accept, support, nurture, strive, share, promise, love, loyal, completely, trust, forever, understand, integrity, true, joy, everlasting, hopeful, eternal, sincerely, soul mate, best friend, spirit, friend, lover, symbol, freedom, teacher, uplift.

Wedding Customs and Traditions

※ ◦◦◦◦◦◦◦◦◦◦ ※

"I promised Antony that even in old age, I would never leave

him alone helpless. And I'm keeping my promise now that

he's facing the health issues he has to face. I will be

there, always, no matter what life may bring."

RICK

These days, both traditional and modern wedding ceremonies include rituals that symbolize the creation of a union.

A compilation of your own personal opinions, principles, culture, and religion will create the overall theme of your wedding. Weddings hold some universal aspects across the globe, but cultures and environment play a critical role in the nitty-gritty details of each ceremony and reception.

Some gay couples will choose to employ traditions from their respective backgrounds, while others will want to take advantage of the fact that there have been no concrete precedents set for gay weddings.

Your wedding is an expression of your and your partner's commitment to each other; therefore, how you express this love has to mesh with your personalities. However, while ingenuity and originality will always thrive in the realm of weddings, you can be assured that even "new" traditions pay homage in some way to the traditions of yesteryear; whether through culture or religion, the wheel is always being reinvented. That's why we give you, in this chapter, past and current traditions adopted by other couples who have entered into matrimonial partnership.

Remember that even with each type of wedding, there are exceptions to the rule. There is nothing wrong with using different components from different traditions to create a truly unique wedding experience.

We would just like to give you the basic overview of some of the religious and cultural traditions from around the world. Feel free to research them more deeply and use elements to create your own invention.

⊶

Christian Wedding Terms and Rituals

The two major branches of Christianity are Roman Catholic and Protestant. The following traditions are derived from both.

✦ VOWS: The point in the ceremony at which the couple declares to one another their commitment to the marriage. There is a formula to follow for specific denominations (i.e. Episcopal, etc.), but vows can be written by the wedding couple in order to personalize the recitation.

✦ PRAYERS OR READINGS: All Christian ceremonies will include readings from the Bible. Some couples will have close family or friends read for them. A priest, minister, or deacon will preside over the ceremony and will also have readings or a sermon to offer.

✦ EXCHANGE OF RINGS: After the "I do's," the couple will place the rings on one another's fingers, thus binding them symbolically.

- EUCHARIST AND WINE: Represents the body and blood of Jesus Christ, offered to the wedding couple on that day; may be followed by a Nuptial Blessing asking for protection and strength.

- UNITY CANDLE: The lit candles denote the Light of the Lord. The couple lights the candle in unison representing their union under the protection of God. They start with two separate candles and end up with one.

At the Reception

There are no absolutes for a Christian wedding reception. The success of any celebration is based on making all your guests feel comfortable, honoring those you want to honor, and having a good time.

Basic components of a wedding reception usually include:

- Receiving line
- Head table
- Food
- Toasts and speeches
- Dancing

Special friends and family may be honored by including them in the receiving line or at the head table. Perhaps you'd like to dance with your grandparents, have your sister make a toast, or have your best friend sing "The Way You Look Tonight." Our Polish friends say their family members would be disappointed if they couldn't dance a polka at family weddings! (Where else will they get a chance to polka?) One New Yorker said the wedding receptions of his family members always have the band play "New York, New York" as the finale. For this family, it wouldn't be right not to see everyone arm in arm trying to do Rockette kicks to "if I can make it there, I'll make it anywhere . . ."

Depending on your commitment to your faith, a priest or minister may be invited to say the blessing before the meal and stay for the remainder of the reception. Your faith may dictate whether to serve alcohol to you guests. It's up to you and your partner to incorporate your tastes and traditions to create a memorable reception.

Jewish Wedding Terms and Rituals

KETUBAH: The marriage contract. Prior to the wedding (or sometimes after), the wedding couple will sign the *ketubah,* which contains promises to each other; it is then read by the rabbi during the ceremony.

YARMULKE: White cap traditionally worn by the rabbi, groom, groomsmen, and male Jewish guests.

HUPPAH: Wedding canopy under which the couple will be married, preferably outdoors. The *huppah* represents God's presence, shelter, and protection. The *huppah* is supported by four poles and ornately decorated with velvet, embroidery, flowers, and greenery. You can make your own *huppah* to personalize your day even more, as long as it is a handmade, temporary structure; the sky is the limit for creating your *huppah.*

SHEVA BERAKHOT: The seven blessings. Usually chanted by the rabbi in Hebrew and English or by honored guests over a cup of wine from which the wedding couple will then take a sip. The blessings celebrate the couple's lifetime together and of happiness to come.

BREAKING OF THE GLASS: At the end of the ceremony, a glass wrapped in cloth or a paper bag is placed on the ground and stomped on amid cheers of "*mazel tov* (good luck)!" While traditionally it was only the groom that did the stomping, new couples are both putting their feet down and participating in this jubilant act together. This act is said to represent a number of ideas, from the destruction of the Holy Temple in Jerusalem to the "shattering" of childhood, to the fragility of the human experience. Finally, the breaking of the glass is sometimes explained as symbolic of the breaking of the bride's hymen.

At the reception

Jewish wedding receptions are joyous celebrations, with much singing and many traditional dances. These dances honor the wedding couple and their guests. A lively Israeli circle dance called the Hora is performed at the wedding reception. While they hold on to either end of a handkerchief, bride and groom are lifted into the air on chairs by their joyful guests, as they are celebrated as king and queen of the night. More guests join in and dance around the couple.

Mitzvah dances are intended for the guests to have a chance to dance with the wedding couple. Below are the dances to honor the guests, where each respective group takes its turn in the middle:

- BUBBES: to honor the grandmothers at the wedding (grandmas in the middle).

- MEHUTONIM: the newly anointed in-laws dance together and mix it up by switching partners.

- FREYLAKH FOR BACHELORS: for all the single men at the reception.

- FREYLAKH FOR BACHELORETTES: for all the single women at the reception.

Highlighted Wedding Customs from Other Religions

Hindu

FLORAL LOVE NECKLACE: A necklace of flowers is exchanged between partners as they ask if the other will join them in a Hindu life together.

FIERY VOWS: The couple performs their vows before a fire in order to be witnessed by God, as the fire represents the divine being. One leads the other around the fire while reciting mantras. A priest professes the seven steps (responsibilities of marriage) as the couple continues to circle around the fire in agreement of these steps.

GATH BANDHAM: A ritual in which a scarf is wrapped around the couple after their hands have been bound together. Family members place their hands on top of the couple's to signify the new family bond.

Muslim

Muslim families of the bride and groom give symbolic gifts to each other as a welcome of each into the family.

MUTUAL MEAL: A meal in which the couple shares with each other foods prepared especially for them.

THE PLEDGE: Similar to exchanging vows, the couple makes a pledge to each other during the ceremony.

Zen Buddhist

THE TEA CEREMONY: One week prior to the wedding, the wedding couple share some alone time by attending a tea ceremony which they prepare together. This is nice quality time they can use to reflect upon the day to come.

FLORAL INCENSE: Symbolizes a person's potential and activates the start of the ceremony.

CLEANSING OF THE MIND: The officiant drops a freshly picked leaf into a container of water. Three drops of this water are placed on the foreheads of the couple. With a dull knife, the officiator removes the water from their foreheads, thus symbolizing the cleansing of their minds and the beginning of their lives together.

Shinto

Traditional Japanese flute music ga ga ku is performed. The Japanese wedding ceremony is conducted by a Shinto priest who first begins by purifying the couple. After the purification and vows are performed, the ancient wedding custom of sharing sake, called *"san san kudo,"* is performed. To close the ceremony, symbolic offerings of small tree twigs called *"sakaki"* are given to the *Kami,* the Japanese spirits or gods.

Cultural Wedding Customs from Around the World

Below are some customs from countries all around the world. Some you may recognize and some may seem downright "foreign" to you.

ROSE CEREMONY: One of the parties hands a white rose to the other, who then places it in a tiny vase with water. The couple then agrees to follow this ritual each year on their anniversary to reaffirm their love for each other. How romantic! Even after years together this simple tradition will enhance any anniversary by evoking the memories of the day you committed yourselves to each other.

HONEY CEREMONY: Using honey to symbolize the sharing of the good, "sweet" side of life, one of the partners dips his/her little finger into the honey and touches the other partner's tongue with it, then vice versa. What a subtle, sensuous, and delicious ritual to incorporate into any type of ceremony to make it truly unique.

CEREMONY OF CANDLES: This is an alternative to the unity candle. The couple begins with one candle representing each of their lives. They proceed to light a third candle which represents their life together. All three candles remain lit to denote their unity and their independent spirits. Unity and independence: We believe that's a balance all couples would like to achieve.

THE FOUR ELEMENTS TASTING: Four flavors are offered to the couple for tasting. The tradition is lemon, vinegar, cayenne, and honey, representing the four tastes that represent the different emotional states in life. This is to say that the couple will stay unified through the bitter, sour, salty, and sweet times. That about covers it—very cool.

EXCHANGE OF KOLA NUTS, AFRICAN: The kola nut is a symbol of healing. Exchanging this symbol is a promise by the couple to be there through the hard times as well as the good. We all need strength through the rough patches in life. This is a fun way to reinforce the promise that you'll weather them together.

HANDFASTING, AFRICAN/CELTIC: In the African tradition, the couple's hands are tied together with a piece of cloth or strand of shells in a representation of their unity. Handfasting is also a Celtic tradition which would occur after the exchanging of rings and vows with the same symbolic representation expressed in the African tradition. So many of the wedding traditions that we've discovered overlap disparate cultures. We really aren't so different, are we?

JUMPING THE BROOM, AFRICAN AMERICAN: The couple sweeps away any bad energy by holding the broom together and sweeping in a circular motion. Then, the broom is placed on the floor and the couple jumps over it together at the count of three. We love this one and the joy that jumping creates. When was the last time you jumped for joy? Give it a try!

HENNA CEREMONY, NORTH AFRICAN, MIDDLE EASTERN, SOUTH ASIAN: The henna ceremony or Mehndi party is held the night before the wedding. Traditionally, it is held in the home of the bride and includes only women from the bride's side. It is a fun and relaxing evening spent applying mehndi (henna) designs to the bride's hands, feet, and anywhere else! Friends and family may also have some mehndi. While applications are being done there may be music, dance, and other entertainment for the guests.

HAND CLEANSING, NATIVE AMERICAN: A jug of water is placed in front of the wedding couple. Each pours water over the other's hands, representing purity of heart and new life together. This humble ritual would be a lovely addition to any ceremony, including one taking place in the Southwest.

CONGREGATIONAL WEDDING CERTIFICATE, QUAKER: After the wedding ceremony, every person in attendance signs the marriage certificate, bearing witness to the couple's union. Our Quaker friends had their certificate written in calligraphy on parchment paper. It was signed in sepia-colored ink by all their guests. They had it matted and framed and it now hangs in a place of honor in their home. It's a true work of art.

EXCHANGE OF COINS, MEXICO: The couple exchanges blessed coins to represent their worth to each other and to convey the security of home and possessions. The ideas of worth and security that are evoked with this blessing make it universal.

RELEASING OF DOVES, PHILIPPINES: A bell-shaped cage holds doves, which symbolize peace and love between the couple, and after the ceremony the couple opens the cage to let the doves free. What can we say—is this a nice touch, or what?

THE POLERBAND, GERMANY: The night before the wedding, family and friends gather at a dinner and rehearsal for the wedding. There is then a performance which dramatizes the future life of the soon-to-be-wed couple. Festivities continue into the evening with dancing, pot-banging, and glass-smashing. The couple then sweeps up the pieces in order to represent the happiness and prosperity to come. Can you imagine what fun this would be?

THE HORSESHOE, ENGLAND: A young woman or girl carries a horseshoe decorated with ribbons while scattering floral petals in front of the bride, all to bring good luck. This is perfect for all you horse lovers.

THE COMMON CUP, GREECE: The couple sips sweet wine three times from a common cup to symbolize their unity. Cheers!

SHUANG XI, CHINA: The Chinese character for happiness, *xi*, pronounced "she," is an important part of Chinese weddings and is usually displayed somewhere at the wedding reception or banquet. The Chinese character combines two individual characters to represent double happiness. Double happiness, or *shuang xi,* signifies good fortune for the newlyweds and ensures a happy future. Just add paper lanterns, chopsticks, and fortune cookies.

These are just a few traditions that could enrich your ceremony. Some even give your guests the opportunity to participate. Find the elements that work for you and incorporate them into your ceremony to create a truly unique experience.

You can mix and match any custom, any ritual, any culture, and any theme. Have fun. If you're African-American and your partner is Jewish, why not jump the broom under the *huppah?* At the reception, serve food from both cultures, or have a Mexican fiesta as a prelude to your honeymoon destination—margaritas, mariachis, tamales, and a piñata!

Wedding Apparel

"The partner who loves you is the one who helps you to know who you really are. I'm so damn lucky I've found that person. I never thought I would."

DANA

Your wedding day is a celebration of two people coming together in a union of love. The emphasis is on the two of you as a unit and most of the day's events will revolve around this concept. However, when it comes to apparel, you have the freedom to express your individuality even as you enter into your lifetime partnership. What you wear can reflect so much about your personality, and this is especially true on your wedding day.

When your average person is asked to think "wedding," what comes to mind are white wedding dresses and black tuxedos. These are the traditional garbs and are still the most popular choices for wedding-day apparel. But wedding styles are no longer restricted to such a small selection, even in the traditional realm.

For one thing, themed weddings are no longer just an offbeat idea. More and more gay and lesbian couples are looking to make their own wedding style unique to themselves and their relationship, thus broadening their scope of what to wear.

One thing to remember is that you will have pictures of this day (in your mind and in your album), so you do want to make sure that you don't pick something you may cringe at ten years from now if you can help it. Fad styles should be avoided unless you are the type of person who revels in "what's hot," and will still take pride in your wedding-day pictures when the style is "way out."

You should be excited to wear what you choose and above all feel comfortable wearing it. If you always dreamed of wearing sparkly black stilettos on your wedding day you'll be comfortable in them—even though they will be far from comfortable—because it's what you've always wanted to wear. After a few walking lessons in them you'll be fine. We hope!

Almost anything goes when it comes to picking your clothes. If there is a theme to your wedding, obviously this theme will dictate the style of your attire. Ever consider a beach-party wedding with bikini-clad brides or clam-digging grooms? We've seen it and it's great. Even if there is no theme, you'll still have a world of options.

For the Brides . . .

A good place to start is to answer the following question: Do you want to wear a dress, a pantsuit, a casual outfit, or something else entirely? If you choose to wear a dress, you'll need to think about whether or not you want to wear something along the lines of the traditional wedding dress. You also have the choice of wearing an evening dress or something as simple as a sundress. If you want to wear a wedding dress but have no idea where to start or how to pick one, buy a few of the latest bridal magazines and you'll more than likely see some styles that appeal to you.

Once you have your style in mind, you can shop around for the best prices. Check your local bridal boutiques or browse online. There are endless choices that come in a wide range of styles and prices. Pinning it down to what it is exactly you want just takes some research.

For sentimental flair, you might want to wear your mother's wedding dress or even your grandmother's wedding dress, if either of them have been preserved. Once you pick a dress, be prepared for alterations and probably at least two fittings. It's all part of making sure your dress looks like it was tailor-made just for you.

If you both decide to wear wedding dresses, you have to decide a few things as well. Do you want to coordinate (with just a little change in the accents of each), or do you want to look totally different from each other? Perhaps you can find similar wedding dresses and incorporate unique accents into each, or even reverse part of the color scheme in a different way on each of the dresses.

One couple we knew actually bought the same wedding dress, one in white and one in cream, and wore different styles of jewelry and hair, and they looked unique yet coordinated. Some brides wear dresses that were as different as night and day. We've also seen one bride wear a gown and the other wear a tux, and because the outfits matched each of their personalities it looked great. The selections ended up being a true representation of themselves and their relationship. (Hey, sometimes opposites attract!)

For the Grooms . . .

The question is whether you want to wear tuxedos, white tie, three-piece suits, casual wear, or something else entirely.

If you choose to wear tuxedos, then you should start looking for your choices preferably at least two months prior to your ceremony.

You can usually get by on a couple of weeks' notice but it's better to be safe than sorry, and to make sure all the alterations are finished on time.

You should start with your local formal-wear shops and actually see some examples of styles you like, or if at all possible, go into a major city nearby (if Barneys isn't right around the corner from you) and go to the larger stores.

The is a very large selection of tuxedos to choose from (semi-formal and formal day to semi-formal and formal evening, and so forth). Unless you are well versed in all of the styles, you'll want to get out and do some shopping to decide what type suits you best. Try the Internet for some additional ideas for styles available.

Maybe you've always dreamed about a certain look, only to find it really doesn't look good on you after you've tried it on. There are definitely different styles to consider and different cuts for different figures. Just as it is with brides and their dresses, so are there many intricacies to consider when expressing your unique style while sporting a tux.

Once you've found the style you like, consider the color, whether you want the two of you in the same color, in opposite colors, or mixing and matching totally unique colors that suit your personalities. The decision is strictly up to the two of you. Many of the weddings we've done had the grooms both dressed in black tuxes with coordinating accessories of different colors (cufflinks, bow ties, cummerbunds, jewelry, studs, etc.) and the same or different flowers on their lapels.

And then there's the occasional wedding where one of the grooms insists on coming in a canary-yellow tux and tails. All part of the personal style of you personally, and you as the second half of a newly joined couple.

———

For Brides and Grooms . . .

Will you be helping to dress your wedding party? If so, you'll need to consider the individual style and body type of each attendant. Picking something that can suit everyone is the goal. You may want to consider picking out a couple of styles to choose from in the same color, and let each attendant pick out the style which best suits him or her, or get into the complexity of mixing, matching, or otherwise coordinating the styles and colors available.

At one male couple wedding we saw the wedding couple in all white, and all of the wedding party in black tuxes (including the women). It was fantastic. Another time all the women in the wedding party were in spectacular black and white dresses and each man was wearing a combination of black and white. The two women (who were getting married) were both in top hats and tails that were a beautiful silver and black combination. Marlene, eat your heart out!

If you choose to let your attendants choose their own attire, please send them shopping with a set of guidelines. This is recommended for wedding parties of more than two. Once you get two or more people picking out what their attire will be, you might end up with—quite literally—a rainbow wedding. But that could also be kind of fun . . . considering who we are, right?

Don't be afraid to express your creativity when it comes to how you will dress on your wedding day. Try to let your personality shine through. Paying strict homage to tradition is an option as well, but don't forget the many other options you have available to you in color and style. Most gay weddings are a perfect mix of both tradition and innovation, and mainstream weddings are taking notice of our new creative philosophy.

Catering Your Affair

"We were up in Alaska, lying out under a starry sky one night.
That's when she turned to me and said, 'You make me
feel like one of those sparkles up there in heaven.
You're the other half of our constellation.'"

AMY

*I*f you're wondering about which areas will be the toughest to tackle, this will probably be your biggest challenge. As we know, it's all about food, isn't it? You can have the most arrestingly beautiful venue with the most stunning floral arrangements and the hottest band, but if the food isn't good, that's ultimately what the guests will focus on.

But in all honesty, even if you're going to have that simple BBQ or clambake, it still might be a good idea for you to read through this chapter just for some pointers. You're still going to have to have somebody make your food (trust us, you do not want to do this yourself) and to serve it. You're also still going to have a bar menu to go with it, since alcohol is usually expected. It is possible (but rarely done) to have a dry wedding. For this type of reception you can create a bar menu composed of popular drinks in virgin form, and other interesting nonalcoholic drinks.

We have tried to break your menu options down into simple categories that are easy to understand. Remember, this can be fun—especially the food tasting part. Menu planning can be just common sense with you both adding to it with your particular tastes. Food choices are unlimited, depending upon the style of your wedding, the location of your event, and a host of other factors.

Catering and Common Sense

Let us give you four hard and fast rules to start with:

1. Never hire a caterer—no matter what—without tasting the food first.

2. Ask the caterer point-blank what the *total* charges are and be firm that you do not want to find that anything has been hidden from you on the day of your wedding. Always find out the *total* per-person cost, including all of the hidden extras like service people, equipment (if offered), bartenders, tax, gratuities, etc.

3. Use our checklist to help you make your decisions along the way. We've tried to make this as easy as possible for you, based on our experience.

4. Shop around for good pricing, recommendations, and professionalism. You will be very glad you did this when all is said and done.

Just a sampling of questions that the caterer should answer:

+ Does the caterer offer package deals in writing?

+ Will there be rental charges for china, silverware, and serving utensils?

+ Are <u>all</u> taxes and gratuities included in the per-person charge?

+ On exactly what date does the final guest count have to be given?

+ Can the caterer supply bartenders if needed?

+ Does the caterer charge a "cake-cutting fee"?

+ What is the customary deposit required?

Now it's time for the two of you to start making your decisions based on what you want. Take a deep breath and work through these choices one at a time. You can always go back and change your mind once you've begun the process of meeting caterers, tasting food, and educating yourself on the options available.

Will your catering be done

+ in house (the location has an on-site caterer)
+ by an independent caterer

Discuss and make a preliminary decision as to what kind of meal you would like to consider and how it will be served:

1. Type of wedding meal:
   + Dinner (with or without appetizers)
   + Cocktails and appetizers only
   + Luncheon
   + Brunch

2. How will the meal be served:

+ A buffet
  served by staff
  informal self-serve

+ Sit-down service with full waitstaff
+ Food stations

3. A choice of:

+ Passed hors d'oeuvres
+ Hors d'oeuvre tables
+ No hors d'oeuvres

(Think carefully on this, especially if there is a time lapse between the ceremony and the reception)

All right! You made it through the most difficult part, believe it or not! You're well on your way to defining what it is the two of you want. Keep in mind as we go through food selection possibilities what your budget will allow you to serve. For the purposes of preliminary food selection, let's just be creative and have fun. Later on you can streamline your choices based on actual per-person or food costs. Remember: There are no rules here, so think creatively when it comes to your food choices.

CHOICE I

Number of Courses

Some of the courses that you can have for your reception include:

Soup, salad, appetizer, pasta, entrées, cheese and fruit, sherbets, additional desserts (not counting the cake), etc.

The most common ones that we've given at our weddings in the inn (and found to be the most successful) have included:

Soup or salad (choice of)

Appetizer

Entrée (choice of either two or three at most)

Wedding cake (dessert)

Decide on the number of courses you want to have before talking to a caterer or location manager.

CHOICE 2
Type of Entrées

We suggest that you make a selection of two entrées (or three at the most) for full sit-down service, more for buffets (depending on the type of meal you want). Choose from the following categories:

- Beef
- Seafood
- Chicken
- Pork
- Lamb
- Vegetarian
- Duck

The top choices at my inn are salmon or sea bass filet (Seafood), filet mignon and rolled chicken breast (see "Recipes").

CHOICE 3
Ethnic Food

If you and your partner have been thinking of doing something different . . . here's your chance.

The Menu: A Few Possibilities

If there are three things that the gay and lesbian community seems to know a lot about, it's travel, food, and wine. I find myself wondering why I'm trying to give suggestions when all of you probably have much more of a sense of food and style than most do. For whatever reason, we tend to excel in the fashion industry, we're major players in the arts and computer fields, and our creative touches are everywhere you look, from San Francisco to New York City to around the globe.

So what does any of that have to do with a discussion of your menu and choosing wines? Because, although I love food and have traveled extensively, I would not presume to tell you what to choose in these categories. I can only offer you some places to begin with, based upon my experiences over the years. I'm sure your palates will discover (or know) what you want, so I'm only here to give some suggestions—take them or leave them.

Over the years, I have relied on my chef, Harry Swavely, to bring out the best in our guests' menu choices. And I'm not alone in that evaluation. In many people's opinions, Harry has never made a dish in the last twenty years that everybody didn't love. His recipes, energetic drive, and knowledge of food were the driving force behind us winning the AAA 4 Diamond Restaurant Award at our inn. He is a wonderful man who loves to cook, and anyone who's had the pleasure of tasting his food is happy that he's still out there in that kitchen.

Harry's philosophy (if I can be so bold as to sum it up) is that if a tried-and-true dish has incredible taste, why does everyone feel the need to keep changing it? He says that part of the art of being a top chef is the ability to create and re-create the same dish once everyone agrees that it's fantastic! Harry knows many award-winning chefs who, although they have limited repertoires, act as if they know it all just because they went to some fancy culinary school. He's told me numerous times that cooking is a lifelong passion and that no one should ever stop trying to learn and grow. If they do, they shouldn't be a chef any longer.

Harry's specialties, beyond everything else that he wonderfully creates, are his desserts. People come here to Bucks County from Philadelphia, New York City, and DC just to have them. Whether it's his warm apple crisp or cranberry bread pudding in the colder months, or his chocolate espresso torte or his award-winning tiramisu, he's established a reputation that is top notch.

What we've done, Harry and I (but mostly Harry), is to put together some of the best recipes that we've offered at the inn for weddings and dinners. They were chosen because any chef worth his salt, as they say, can make them from our menu choices here. They are simple and easy to serve, but incredible in their taste, and sure crowd pleasers. (See "Recipes" for detailed recipes.)

We've included one hot and one cold soup for you to sample, depending on the season of your wedding. We picked the best-loved salads we had—three of them in total. We've also included warm Brie with apple chutney if you fancy something different. The entrées include the filet, the pistachio encrusted sea bass, and the duck with cherry sauce (our three biggest favorites). There are also three others that everyone seems to love, including our crab cakes, our rolled chicken breast with fortina cheese, and our braised Norwegian salmon.

Remember that this is just a starting point for you. Try these dishes in a taste test if you want. If you decide to serve something else wonderful at your wedding reception, maybe then you'll just try these recipes yourselves for dinner one night. Harry would love to think that there are people out there who appreciate his art.

I've also included, although you'll be having your cake, his recipe for cranberry bread pudding. That's what I consider a perk for you. Try it sometime, for a little sampling of one of Harry's staple desserts.

The Sample Menu comes first, followed by some notes on wines, bar service, and seating. Happy Tasting! (And Harry says *Bon Appetit!*)

Wedding Menu Sample

STARTERS

Soup (Potato Leek or Chilled Gazpacho)

Salad (Fig and Stilton Salad or Warm Goat Cheese Salad)

or

Warm Brie with Apple Chutney

ENTRÉES

Filet Au Poivre

Pistachio Encrusted Sea Bass

Duck with Cherry Sauce and Mushroom Compote

Rolled Chicken Breast with Prosciutto and Fontina Cheese

Crab Cakes

Braised Norwegian Salmon with Fig Glaze

A Few Other Tips

✦ If your wedding budget is tight, consider a dish like the rolled chicken breast with fontina cheese. Stay away from the higher-priced items like the filet mignon. If your budget is really tight, consider having just a cocktail reception with cake and passed hors d'oeuvres.

✦ Find out what dishes are your caterer's specialty. Choose entrées that have a broad appeal, whether a fish, chicken, or meat.

- Be sure that your caterer can include a vegetarian plate if it's requested.

- An afternoon wedding with a brunch or lunch will be cost saving to you.

- Your hors d'oeuvres should be a combination of hot and cold (see suggestions in Recipes chapter) and should, if at all possible, be passed, as well as at stations. (Stations are helpful to those who miss the waiters when they whiz by.)

- Most caterers have complimentary tastings for the wedding couple. You might want to take that one step further (if your budget allows), pay for his time and invite friends or family whose opinions you trust to the tasting. It's a great way to get feedback and have a wonderful dinner party at the same time.

Alcohol and Drinks

If there's anything that we've learned at the inn about cost savings for the wedding couple, it's to focus on your selection of wines and the extent of the bar service you need for your reception.

If you are one of those couples who expect to have an open bar for the duration of your reception, with premium drinks being constantly served, expect to pay premium price. All facilities have to guesstimate, in some form or other, how much of a drinking crowd you will have with you, unless of course they keep a running bar tab on every drink made.

If your crowd doesn't drink too heavily, of course, you'll save money. Another option is to have a cocktail hour (keep it limited) and then a champagne toast, and then follow with wines at dinner. The great part about this option is that you limit the alcohol intake, which might be a good thing when you consider how much you'll end up paying.

We've found that our couples have loved the idea of saving money and not letting their guests get too intoxicated, and were able to afford higher quality wines because they just stuck with an open cocktail hour. It has been the most often-used setup we've had at the inn.

Some facilities also allow you to bring your own liquor, which means that you can save yourself a considerable amount of money by buying it wholesale. If you're going to go this route make sure you start with the staples and go from there (gin, vodka, whiskey, etc.).

The Champagne Cocktail . . .
Our Signature Drink

The favorite drink for our guests was our champagne cocktail, made from an eighteenth-century family recipe. After the cocktail hour, we would serve trays of it for the toasting, and sometimes again at the end of the night.

Strawberries and banana pieces are soaked in champagne over night in the refrigerator. Added to the mixture is a smaller amount of grand marnier and brandy. Then, just before serving, additional champagne is added to the base of this mixture. It is poured from pitchers into glasses with a half strawberry and slice of banana. People love it, and it has an incredible mellowing effect on the guests—in a good way! Allow for a couple of glasses of champagne cocktail for each guest to toast the evening with.

Choosing Wines

If you and your partner already have a red and white wine that you love or that has a sentimental value to you, by all means consider using it. It would be hard here to condense in a few paragraphs the "art of wine" that takes years to develop. Consider asking a trusted friend, your local wine-shop merchant, or even your caterer for advice if you lack knowledge in this area.

Usually guests are evenly split on which to drink, red or white, and your choice will also depend on the food that you are serving for dinner. Chardonnay (in the most simplistic terms) is a very popular white that works well at dinner receptions, just as Cabernet or Merlot is a popular red to serve with meats.

Try to find someone who is knowledgeable in wines and who you trust to help you choose. Prices vary greatly and usually you can expect to get five glasses to a bottle. Make sure the waitstaff does not overfill the glasses, which is a no-no for any connoisseur of fine wines. Your caterer should be a valuable resource to you in your selections—they've probably done many parties and know something about the choices you can make.

Remember: wine has been used and enjoyed for centuries to celebrate all of life's special occasions.

Seating

We've tried to stay away from those old traditional wedding suggestions as much as possible, so that you can feel creative and free, but this may be one area where you would do well to be careful before throwing caution to the wind. Unless your wedding reception is a very small affair, it would probably be a good idea to have seating arrangements for your tables.

There are a couple of good reasons for holding on to this particular traditional way of thinking. For one thing, you don't want those that are closest to you to be stuck out in the far reaches of the galaxy where nobody gets a chance to see them. Then there's the case of the old girl-friend/new girlfriend or old boyfriend/new boyfriend deciding to sit right next to the old partner. And what about Aunt Bessie who ends up sitting right next to the blasting speakers and can't hear a word anyone's saying? With a little bit of organization and forethought this seating assignment thing shouldn't have to push you over the edge while you're trying to create a happy time for all.

Your first step is to make a map of the room, including major fixtures like support columns, bars, dance floor, etc. Draw in the tables, showing the number of people sitting at each. Remember, your cocktail friends are going to love you if you seat them close to that bar!

Here are a few guidelines for you to consider as you start to make your seatings. If they don't work for you, adapt them for your needs or just throw them out entirely. They're just general guidelines.

- Don't sit divorced or separated couples together. Maybe it sounds stupid to even mention this, but we've been to two weddings where that little guideline was forgotten and a few fireworks ensued.

- Seat your closest friends closest to you. Most wedding guidebooks will say that this includes your family too. We all know that sometimes our adopted friends are much closer to us than our family. This one we leave up to you. A word of caution, though: you might want to think twice before you ruffle any feathers by putting your brother or sister way in the back next to the bathroom. Remember that we don't have to follow traditional lines. Do what you think is best, but obviously don't ever intentionally hurt anyone's feelings if you can help it.

- Split up the main wedding party however you'd like to. (This is a big departure from traditional wedding protocol. There have been volumes written on the etiquette of bridal party seating.) As far as we're concerned, there's only rule that applies here . . . you stick with your partner!

- If you want to have one large table for the whole party, fine, but consider splitting yourselves off into smaller groups of two or four. (This assumes that there are more than just the two of you in the bridal party to begin with.)

- Let your attendants sit with their partners if it can be done. This keeps everyone much happier in the long run. Consider seating one bridal party member with their partner at each table. Everyone feels more included in the festivities when they have a member of the party sitting with them.

- Try to assign seating by tables, usually two or four people to a table, up to a maximum of eight. That way the couples can see where they're sitting by table, not by chair, and discover for themselves what is the best combination for socializing. The easiest way to do this is to have place cards on a tray as they enter with their table number next to their name. For weddings over forty-nine or so people, there should also be a seating chart on the tray.

- On each table there should be a larger card which corresponds to the table number. You can also set cards at each place setting if you want to define the specific seats, but guests do like to find their name and table on their own and see who's sitting there before they find their place to sit.

Note: Be sure to bring along some extra place cards for any last-minute confirmations that have to be seated.

When you're making your table assignments, try to find a spot for each person at a table where they'll have something in common with other guests sitting there. This takes a little time and energy, but wouldn't you like it if someone took the time to think about you and whom you might pair up with for a wonderful evening? It's a matter of stepping in your guests' shoes for a bit and caring that they end up having a good time.

Beware of what's known as the "head tables." This is where the worst in your closest family and friends can come out if they feel passed over. You don't want to slight anyone, but it's your wedding and you get to choose who ultimately goes where. Be considerate, though, of those who are disabled or elderly.

In situations where you think a close friend might be hurt because they're not sitting up front, let them know ahead of time about the situation. If they're a good friend, they're going to understand. Besides, it's not like you won't be seeing them out on that dance floor!

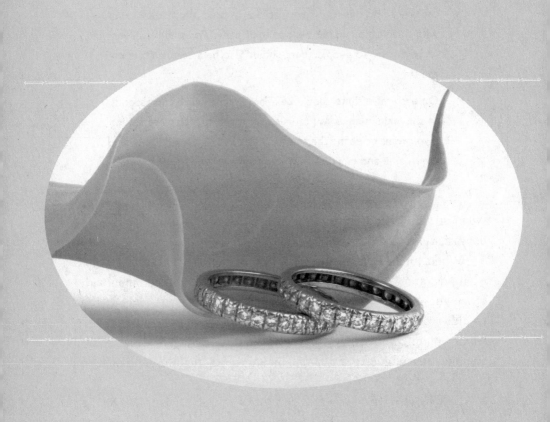

About Contracts

> *"I promised myself that I wanted to help those around me
> and to search for the knowledge in life. Yet, I knew that I
> needed someone special to help fill an empty longing
> in my soul. He just suddenly walked into my life one
> day, and my life will never be the same."*
>
> THOMAS

A contract, simply put, is a legal agreement that is put down in writing. It is usually coupled with a monetary deposit in some form. As you make arrangements, you will likely enter into several agreements with the florist, caterer, and the like.

If there is nothing else you get out of this chapter, please remember to read and understand everything in your contracts, especially the fine print. Make sure everything the two of you want is specifically spelled out. It will save you a lot of wasted time, money, and anger if you follow this guideline. Sometimes, in your rush to get things done, you may agree to something verbally, only to have it later forgotten by the other party. Whatever is agreed upon in your meetings, be sure to write it down!

When you make your location arrangements, book the caterer, the florist, or the photographer, or order your attire, be sure to have a specific contract spelling out *exactly* what you are agreeing to. It is worth the extra time it takes, because the last thing you want is to have the unexpected arise an hour before your wedding takes place.

Keep all of your contracts and receipts in your wedding briefcase, or other safe place.

When you have your first consultations with these professionals, don't be embarrassed that you're jotting down the main points of your discussions. Refer to these notes later and make sure they are put into your contract, clearly spelled out.

Do **not** leave anything to chance; be *specific* in all of your dealings. Sometimes it might feel laborious or petty to insist upon crossing every "t" and dotting every "i," but it could save you unnecessary time lost and undue stress later on. Contracts are standard procedure and they should be detailed and completed to the satisfaction of both parties.

It is also imperative that you read *all* of the fine print in every contract. If you are not good at this, have your partner, a trusted family friend, or best of all, your attorney look them over if you are unclear about anything in the contract.

Unclear contracts (with nonspecifics) can severely hurt couples that are getting married when they find out that important things were not explicitly defined. This can cause a great deal of heartache and tears on a special day that was meant to be only memorable in good ways!

Always read all of the details of the *cancellation policies, fees, and refunds*.

All contracts, generally speaking, should include:

+ The exact time, date, and year of the wedding

+ Refund policies for both the vendor and the client

- A negligence/misconduct clause which covers both parties

- The date the contract was signed

- The time the vendor should be there (and when it is all to be set up)

- The date and times of any deliveries that are necessary

- Emergency contact numbers (and/or cell phone numbers)

- Everything detailed in specific line/item breakdowns

- Everything that was mutually agreed upon

- Total cost for *all* services as outlined, with no hidden items

- Clear explanations of any and all grace periods that are or are not offered

- The deposit amount and date paid, and balance amount and date to be paid

- An insurance liability clause with specifications

When in doubt, ask your attorney and then write it out! That's the rule. Don't leave anything to chance. We cannot stress this enough!

Most of the contracts that wedding vendors offer are stock form contracts. Feel free to write anything that you feel is important into that contract and have both parties—yourself and the vendor—initial alongside to indicate that you both accept the more clearly defined terms and conditions. Be sure to clear this with the vendor before you write on the existing contract so you do not risk making that existing contract void.

In the case of unfinished details (details that have not yet been finalized on the contract), state on the contract that they will be confirmed in writing by a specified date. Also consider adding a maximum amount clause in such specific cases.

If you have questions or doubts about any details, make sure you talk to your attorney. Never proceed blindly when it comes to contracts.

Finding Gay-Friendly Vendors

"After being together for thirty-two years, we've both learned that we can keep love in our house if both of us find peace and love in ourselves first."

HARRY

For the last four years, GayWeddings.com has been searching out gay-friendly wedding vendors. We've learned a thing or two along the way and we've met wonderful people who stood up for our community at times when it wasn't a popular cause. We suggest you look into our vendor directory pages to see who's listed near you, but we'd also like to throw out some suggestions, too.

It's very important that you feel totally at home with the people who are helping you with your affair. The last thing you want on your wedding day is some waiter or valet parker who has a negative attitude about who you are. This chapter will offer some tips that might help you make important decisions when it comes to wedding vendors, locations, and other vital elements for your wedding.

How to Find Friendly Vendors

Gay couples must tackle one extra step when hiring their wedding vendors and services. Before getting into any particular vendor's capabilities and quality of work, they must figure out whether or not this person or organization is gay-friendly. "Gay-friendly" obviously means that they are not negatively prejudiced against a person's gay or lesbian lifestyle.

Sometimes it seems like an intimidating task, but it really helps if the two of you go into this fully prepared, remembering that there is still, unfortunately, a stigma surrounding the issue of gay weddings. Sad to say, but it still remains true that gay couples will not always be met with a warm greeting. Here are a couple of steps to take in order to find vendors that are friendly and happy to have your business.

1. The Internet is probably the best place to start. GayWeddings.com has a comprehensive database covering the whole of the U.S., and there are scores of other gay-related websites that list resources on a local level. Of course, you'll learn that finding gay-friendly vendors may be easier for couples living in say, San Francisco than it would be for couples living in a small town in Alabama. However, if you seek . . . you shall find. If you do not readily have Internet access, then move to the next step.

2. Use your local phone book and/or wedding guides. Simply make a phone call to the vendor in question and ask:

   a. Would they offer their services to a gay couple for a gay wedding?

b. Have they rendered their services at other gay weddings in the past?

   You will more than likely be able to tell by the answers and the tone of voice whether or not this vendor is seriously gay-friendly. You can firm up your hunches in subsequent interviews. If they have done a gay wedding in the past, that's great, but if not don't rule them out completely. Continue a dialogue with them to see how compatible you are with them. You could be this vendor's first gay wedding and you could reap the rewards of their determination to create an awesome event.

3. Make sure you have contracts that are very specific with anyone who is connected with essential parts of your affair. Question them and be satisfied that they (and their staff) are professional.

4. Double-check that the contracts have everything spelled out exactly the way you want it, including all of the details, times and dates, and anything that you don't want.

5. Be up front with them about the type of affair you're having. I asked everyone point-blank, before hiring them, whether or not they had any problems in helping to organize gay weddings. If they did, I gave them the opportunity to express it up front and knew where they stood beforehand. I once had a caterer's assistant say he would prefer not to be involved. I thanked him, muttered under my breath something about his narrow-mindedness, and was glad that at least he said it then and didn't wait until my special day to express himself.

6. Ask other couples who have had their ceremonies who they used. This is a great resource. Even neighbors and people who work with you in the office may have a suggestion to follow up on.

7. If you're thinking about an inn for the ceremony or reception, go to our website GayFriendlyInns.com where, so far, we list almost a thousand inns across the country.

8. Interview whomever you're considering over the phone. Don't hesitate to ask questions—we can't stress this enough. Schedule

interviews and property tours and have your list of questions prepared ahead of time.

9. Be discerning and go as a couple, or if you're choosing a vendor on your own, take someone with you whose judgment you trust. They'll be looking out for your best interest and can probably help you to make a wise decision.

10. If you can, meet any additional staff that will be working for you the day of the wedding to be sure that they are comfortable and will make your guests feel welcome. Understand that for some, this may be their first gay wedding. If they seem open and appear to be caring people, chances are that they will be moved when you take your vows, just as all of your family and friends will be touched in wonderful ways when they see your love expressed.

Remember: you are employing these people and part of their employment includes the requirement that they have a high level of professionalism. It's not too much to ask that they treat you with respect and dignity at all times and not have attitude. We've found, in our experience, that the more people learn about the issue of gay weddings, and meet the wonderful people from our community, the more they come to understand and respect who we are and what we're really about.

Flowers and Florists

"Part of the agreement for us, when we agreed to marry,
was that we would never step on each other's freedom
to be whoever each of us were. Because of that,
we've continued to let each other grow and our
possibilities together still seem infinite."

PATRICK

lowers are one of the most vital elements you will need
to choose for your ceremony. Whether it is just simple
boutonnières for your lapels, roses clustered in a bou-
quet, potted palms scattered around by the dining/bar
area, a single bud in a vase on the table, or something much more elaborate, flowers will bring color, vibrancy, and romance to your event.

You'll want to start at the venue you've booked to see if flowers are
included. Many times they will include floral centerpieces or other

small tokens. From there, you might want to consult with a floral designer. Most florists will offer this service to help you design a floral concept or look for your wedding. Another option which many couples choose is to design the floral scheme by themselves.

If neither of you is gifted in the area of floral design—which hardly seems possible considering the stereotype straight America seems to have when they think of our community—don't get all bent out of shape over it. You certainly know friends who are gifted at decorating and arranging, or you can always hire a professional to oversee it. It's just important that you have an overview of some of the principles of floral design and understand the effect these elements will have on the look and feel of your ceremony and reception.

Here are a few suggestions on where to start and how to decide what might work for you. We've done many weddings before where the flowers were picked from our gardens or purchased at the flower farms nearby and arranged by our staff, with the most creative person overseeing the project.

If you're one of those fortunate couples having your ceremony in a natural setting like a park or beside a lake, you may not have to put a lot of thought into flower arrangements. But we would still like you to consider having at least one huge vase, strategically placed in just the right spot. Even in these wonderful settings you should also consider the flowers you'll need for personal adornment and what blooms you'll want for your reception.

We've tried to make it simple for the two of you to get your creative juices flowing by going through the following list. Talk with friends, arrange a couple of appointments with recommended florists, and make it happen. Odds are that one of you, at least, can certainly do this. If not, call on those people you trust and give them the ideas you've jotted down from the list to get their feedback. Your ceremony and reception can only be richer because of it!

Creative Florals

   a. Visit at least two large flower farms or florist shops in your area. Bring a small spiral notebook with you to jot down your favorites. Ask to see any books they may have on wedding flowers, including arrangements and centerpieces.

   b. In your notebook, jot down the following to consider:

1. Our favorite flowers are _____

2. Our favorite filler plants are _____

3. When it comes to flowers, the colors that seem to complement our location and wedding colors are. . . .

     . . . *matching shades of* _____
     . . . *contrasting shades of* _____

4. When we think about what we're going to wear and our location, we visualize using the following the most:

     Soft white shades with some pastels
     Mostly similar shade tones
     Brilliant color blooms
     Bright, offbeat shades of yellow, orange, purple, etc.

5. In our imagination, when we think of arrangements, we tend to see

     Elaborate arrangements
     Natural, more simple arrangements

6. We agree that roses should be a primary flower used

     Yes   No

7. When we think of the table centerpieces, we see

     Large arrangements
     Small arrangements
     Topiaries
     Other _____

8. For fillers in flower arrangements, we like

    Ferns

    Grasses

    Blooming Branches

    Stick branches

    Boxwood

    Baby's Breath

    Ivy

9. Some of the flowers that are in season for our wedding that we like are _____

    (These flowers can represent tremendous savings, since flowers are always cheaper when plentiful.)

10. We've decided that flowers will play an important part for us in the following

    Bouquet

    Arrangements

    Wedding Arch or Gazebo

    Pews or Aisle

    Boutonnières

    Altar or place we stand for ceremony

    Table centerpieces

    Bar area

    Entrance area

11. After looking over our location(s) we think we might need the following number of. . .

    . . . arrangements _____

    . . . table centerpieces _____

    (Write in your notebook where you see placing them and their size.)

12. For last-minute filler arrangements, we see using the following

    Orchids

    Dahlias

    Lilies

Hydrangeas
Tulips
Peonies
Lily of the Valley
Herbs
Wildflowers
Lilacs
Gardenias
Others

13. We need a flower-covered arch or *huppah*

   Yes   No

14. We've calculated the number that we will need of the following

   Boutonnières (for attendants, family, ushers, etc.)
   Corsages
   Bouquets
   Floral Wreaths

15. We would like to have a flower girl carry a basket full of petals

   Yes   No

Some parting thoughts on flowers

+ CONTRACTS: Make sure the contract has everything you've dis-
  cussed written down, including all of the details, the types of
  flowers to be used, and the exact number and size of all arrangements and table centerpieces. The contract should detail all
  charges, including extra fees such as setup. It should also include
  drawings or approximate numbers of all arrangements and other
  items such as *huppahs,* garlands, and arches, etc.

+ DELIVERY: Make sure to have one of your attendants, a friend,
  or responsible family member be there when the flower delivery

and setup begins. Check for freshness and that your whole order has been filled. (The flowers should be there and all set up before any photos are taken.) Keep them out of the sun and heat as much as possible and be sure that they are misted.

+ Keep in mind that the key to enhancing your ceremony and reception with flowers is to know what you are trying to achieve. Learn what sizes, colors, and designs are going to enhance what you're trying to create.

+ Make the decision about whether you want the florals to be kept at a minimum or to be lavish. Do you want them to follow traditional lines or not?

+ When you're trying to find someone to help with your planning, always trust your instincts on whether their vision is matching yours, and how well they listen.

+ Make sure you go through the books they have to offer, or go to a library or bookstore and look for photographs of the look you're searching for.

+ Be certain that all the details are in the contract, and before you sign, be as certain as possible of their reliability.

+ If you are working on a tight budget, make sure that your vendors are giving you the best they can for the money you're spending.

+ A florist that offers full service and setup can be your greatest ally, but be realistic about whether or not this can fit into your budget. If you can afford it, these professionals can make a fair location look stunning, and a great location fabulous.

An unforgettable wedding, no matter how small, is all in the details. Flowers are the crowning touch that makes the occasion memorable.

The Wedding Cake

———————————

"I come from the Midwest. I was brought up to be what they all call a man's man: tough, rugged, standing on my own two feet. I've been in construction all my life . . . am I giving you a clear enough picture of me? If anyone would have ever told me even five years ago that I'd be standing up with another man at an altar, I probably would have beaten the crap out of him. Look at me now. I don't apologize for it. Standing up there with him at that altar was probably the smartest thing I've ever done in my life!"

JAKE

The best cakes not only look fantastic, creating *oohs* and *ahhs,* but they taste incredible too.

It's best to decide on the type of cake you'd like after you've decided on your style, colors, flowers, and decorations. This way you can incorporate all of your main design elements into this detail of your reception, creating a real show-stopper dessert!

When selecting your cake, keep in mind that there are pastry chefs who specialize only in wedding cakes. Because of their years spent in the field, their expertise far exceeds a baker who doesn't specialize. These cake designers approach their work with passion, artistry, and pride.

If you have any fabric swatches of your color scheme, the baker may use them for inspiration in his design. The cake should be a component of the whole theme and style you're creating, standing out, yet working in perfect combination with all the other details.

Don't hesitate to request tasting samples from cake designers before making your final choice. Previewing cakes is a delectable rite of passage for every engaged couple. Your tastings should include the cake itself, the icing, and the fillings that might be included. There is nothing worse than seeing a beautiful wedding cake and then finding out it has no taste, or worse yet, a taste that you don't like. Remember that you have to try to please the palates of many guests. The cakes that have the greatest mass appeal are vanilla pound cake, chocolate-chip pound cake, and sponge cake.

If you just can't live without your favorite double-chocolate almond cake with raspberry filling and lemon icing, then consider having a smaller one of that flavor made to serve or put away for a private celebration after the wedding. But this is your day and if you have a particular favorite that is not the norm, by all means, go for it! Even though it's nice to be able to please the majority with a safe bet, something more exotic or creative might be good enough to impress many of your guests and introduce them to something new—just another nice way for them to remember your special day. Plus, if it's your favorite it can't be all that bad, right? Just make sure your partner agrees.

Generally speaking, a cake price is based on the number of slices and the time and effort that it takes to make it. Cakes can range anywhere from two dollars to seventeen dollars a slice! If you need to budget here, consider having a smaller cake with additional tiers made of Styrofoam that are decorated in the same icing as the edible layer. Another cost saver is to have a sheet cake decorated with real fruit and flowers (free of pesticides, of course). Handmade flowers of sugar, unique shapes, and basket-weave icing patterns add tremendously to the price. Another cost saving device is to serve smaller portions and cut down on the size of cake that you will need. If you're having a large wedding (over a hundred guests), think twice before having Mom make the cake to save money. I'm sure she's a great baker, but it takes years of expertise to become a cake designer and the results are worth hiring a pro.

In most cases, butter cream frosting is less costly than fondant frosting, and it has a wonderful taste. The downside is that butter cream frosting does not allow for that smooth, flat surface that traditional cakes have become known for. Some of the finest-tasting cakes use a combination of the two frostings, one for taste, and the other for design.

Most cake designers agree, when talking tiers, that five or more layers are needed for over 175 guests, and three tiers should serve approximately sixty to a hundred guests, with generous portions.

There are three main types of cakes: sheet (one layer), stacked (layers lying one on top of the other), and column (columns between layers). The grander the cake, the more columns are added.

Be sure to find a topper for the cake that you both like. It can be anything from a porcelain family heirloom, to fresh or artificial flowers, to a piece of spun sugar made into a design that you've created yourself. Yes, they do make toppers with two brides or two grooms; in fact, they have been one of the top sellers at GayWeddings.com's wedding boutique. Your cake designer will have many suggestions for you to choose from, and don't hesitate to ask other couples that you know what they did at their wedding.

The table that the cake sits on can be almost as important as the cake itself. Use fabric and decorations that coordinate with your color scheme and the colors of your cake, or choose white or off-white and simple greens to make the cake stand out even more. The table can be round, oval, or square or it can echo the shape of the cake. Consider having the cake designer help you with this so the table becomes part of their display. The delivery of the cake must be timed perfectly and agreed upon beforehand so that the cake table can be in place and completely decorated before the cake's arrival.

The creativity of cake making can fill volumes. Cascading ribbons and flowers of icing, choices in layering and design, and specialty surfaces, smooth or textured, all create an art form that is limitless. The cake and design that you choose will create a lasting impression on your guests. Make it unique and a reflection of both of your tastes. Your cake is one of the biggest highlights of your wedding, and it can be the most fun to create.

Note: Cakes are traditionally cut by the couple toward the close of the reception while the dancing is still going on. If you have a DJ to announce that the event is about to happen, all the better. If not, either your parents, one of your attendants, or one of you can make the announcement by tapping your silverware on a glass. Make sure you get photos of the moment. The cutting of the cake should be the culmination of a day you'll never forget.

Cake Information Sheet

(Include this information in your notebook, along with your contract)

Cake Designer _____

Address _____

Phone Numbers _____

Cell (Emergency) _____

Number of Slices _____ Filling _____

Icing Type _____

Topper Type _____

Number of Tiers _____ Flavor _____

Total Price (including setup, accessory rentals, and delivery)
$

Accessory Rentals Included

Deposit $ Balance $

Delivery Date

Specific Time (per contract)

Music, Bands, and DJs

"So she's says to me, 'I don't care. I want you to carry me over

the threshold.' Look at me . . . I'm just a little thing.

And Mary's a big girl, by any standards. She'd be the first to

admit it. We ended up falling over the railing into the rose

bushes on the side of the porch! We picked thorns out of our

behinds for the first hour of our damn honeymoon!

Leave it to Mary to have the bright ideas."

DORIS

The whole mood for your wedding and reception can be set by the music you play. Your choices can include a classical guitarist, a bagpiper, a harpist, a jazz combo, a keyboard player, a rock band, an eight-piece orchestra, or a DJ with pre-programmed selections you've made. Then there is the choice of what will be played at the wedding, the reception, or both. You and your partner's personal taste, venue, and budget will be the deciding factors. The music at the ceremony and the reception should be a reflection of who you are as a couple.

Make sure that you don't hire anyone until you've heard them play or listened to any CDs they may have, and you've been told that you can personalize their selections to suit your taste. Be sure to ask for references, especially from other couples at whose weddings they've played. If they have any videos of performances, make sure to see them. Don't hesitate to call their references.

To give you a general ballpark figure for music, if you're not just going to play "Here Comes The Bride" off a cassette tape, the rate usually will be from around eighty dollars up to $275 an hour for each musician. Remember, this is just a general amount. It will vary greatly by region. There may be certain times during your ceremony when it would be appropriate to use a song from your favorite CD. This can also be a cost-saving measure for the two of you.

It is very important that you make sure that the musicians are sheltered at all times from weather. Instruments are very expensive and musicians guard them with their lives.

There are basically four main places during the ceremony for music in traditional weddings. We're not saying you have to follow this rule just because it's always been done that way. It's just good to know the basics and apply your creativity from there. The ceremony music breaks are as follows:

The Prelude

When: Before the wedding starts, while the guests are being seated, and until the actual ceremony begins. The prelude starts as soon as the first guests arrive. This music will set the tone and the mood from the very beginning.

The Processional

When: When the wedding party is coming down the aisle. It is the music during which the grand entrance was traditionally made by the bride. In our case, it can be two brides or two grooms, and it can be done with or without the drama and flair. March music is usually played for the processional, but it can be adapted in any creative way the same-sex couple sees fit.

The Interludes

When: Occur while the ceremony is taking place. The idea behind this music is to highlight certain parts of the ceremony, for example, the unity candle lighting or ring exchange. It can be a classical or singer's solo, or a song that has great meaning to the two of you.

Note: Please don't overdo this, okay? You're supposed to allow the guests see the love you two have for each other, but please be careful not to make it too contrived or too damn long. (It's been known to happen on occasion!) It would be a mistake to do so and nobody wants to wear out their guests at the very start. A little music goes a long way. Just be genuine and find songs that have a special meaning to you both.

The Recessional

When: Takes place as the wedding couple and attendants start to leave. It should be very festive and happy, and should include some drama and flair, reflecting who the two of you are as a newly joined couple (without going overboard of course). It's your chance to have your guests sitting on the edge of their seats in anticipation of what may be coming up next!

Talk with your partner and figure out what suits you both. From there, take into consideration the space in which the musicians will be playing, your budget, the theme of your event, and how the music will reflect both of your personalities.

As you make your musical selections, remember that variety can be the spice of life, especially in this instance. Your guest list will probably be made up of a great variety of people. Consider the options of songs and beats and choose a wide range of fast and slow songs, old standards and new hits, etc.

Let your music set the stage. You can have the lead band member or DJ become the master of ceremonies and create a beautiful ambiance if he or she is a great show person. When making your decisions about the music for your ceremony and the music or performers for your reception, always go back to the idea of what you are trying to create. What emotions do you want to bring out in your guests? From the heavenly sounds of a lone harpist to the heightened excitement of a great rock and roll band to the heartfelt solo given by a great singer, music can have a profound impact on what you are trying to achieve with your celebration.

Here are a few reminders to keep in mind while the two of you are researching the music and musicians you want to have:

+ Make sure that your location space has room for the type of music you're considering.

+ Also be sure that the location allows for amplified music (check for noise restrictions) and has access to the power source you'll need.

+ Disc jockeys are usually quite a bit less expensive than bands or other professionally trained musicians. Their fees usually begin at about four hundred dollars and up for a four to five hour reception. They usually have a wonderful mix of music that can appeal to all of the age groups. If done well, DJs can keep the party mood upbeat and flowing throughout your celebration.

+ When looking for a band, remember that prices will vary depending on how long they are expected to play, the season of the year, and the number of members you need.

+ Make certain that the band, musicians, or DJs have no qualms about you having a request list of songs to play. You should consider compiling that list for them to see before you meet with them.

Music, if chosen well, will set the tone and mood for your whole day. It is the soul of life. Give your guests a glimpse into what your two souls are like, now that they are joined.

At the Reception

This is where the music gets good. The most common choice for weddings is either a DJ or a live band that plays pop favorites. Most DJs or bands have extensive play lists and will incorporate the Top 40 into the specified list of your choice. You can pick the set list from the first song to the last song if you like. Do you love Elvis? Or prefer disco? Only want punk rock? Or maybe show tunes? By talking with your DJ or band beforehand, you'll know whether or not they can tailor their play list exactly to your design.

It's true that most of the time, couples will not pick out a play list from start to finish. Usually current popular music is on tap, unless a specified theme is stressed or the couple has very particular tastes. A large portion of the musical night can be left up to the requests of guests, which is always fun for them. Most of the time, the couple will pick out the songs to play during special dances or moments during the reception.

Some traditional dances that you may want to consider (or steer completely clear of) can include:

THE FIRST DANCE: This is the first time the brides or grooms will dance together as a married couple. If there is a song that you consider "your song," then this would be the time to play it.

THE PARENTS' DANCE: Guys, this is the time to dance with Mother; gals, this is the time to dance with Dad.

THE ELECTRIC SLIDE, CHICKEN DANCE, OR MACARENA: Group dances. These dances are beloved and hated by millions of wedding guests around the world. Even though these dances may have seen their heyday, some weddings just don't seem complete without them.

Whether or not you have group dances, and whether you play Top 40 or disco, remember that the reception is what your guests will remember the most and that music creates the mood for the celebration. If you can get those guests out of their seats and dancing, the fun only increases and it's likely your wedding will be one of life's memorable events.

Photographers

"When I let myself give love and kindness to my partner, it makes her feel loved and cared for. I know it does. The miracle is that it always rebounds back to me, multiplied."

SUZANNE

The photographer will be responsible for creating memories that will last a lifetime for you and your partner. The album they create should reflect who your are as a couple, and your story together.

Even if you're budget conscious, this is one area that we recommend not cutting down on too much and definitely not cutting out completely. Your pictures will be a priceless memento of one of the most important days of your life. We have heard too many stories of couples who were disappointed with the work of their photographers, or who regretted not hiring a professional in the first place. Your cousin Kate might take great photos in her photojournalism class, but if she is emotionally involved in the day (the category under which pretty much anyone you would invite would fall), then it probably is not a good idea to enlist her for shooting your wedding. You really need to hire someone who can shoot an objective view of your day.

In order to find a reputable photographer, be sure to ask family and friends for recommendations. Look at the work each photographer has done in their portfolio. See how they use lighting and color and images to create their best shots. Find the candid photos and posed shots you like best and note how they were taken if you'd like similar shots yourself.

The personality of your photographer is very important since they will always be close by during your wedding and the reception to follow. They will be working behind the scenes as you both get ready, and will also have a lot of contact with your guests, family, and friends. The photographer should have a relaxing and welcoming personality, one that makes people feel comfortable.

Make sure they're not the type that's going to be hanging out at the bar. Any indication that this might occur is a sure sign you should start looking for somebody else! Make certain that you call their references and that they include at least two sets of wedding couples for you to speak to. Question the references about the photographer's professional performance.

If there are any photographic effects that you are especially fond of, make sure they can create them. Also be sure that they have back-up equipment in case something goes wrong with their first set of cameras or lenses.

You will not only be paying for your photographer's time, but also for your pictures. Be very clear on what the cost will be right up front. If they are creating albums for you and your family (upon request), know what additional costs will be incurred. Ask about the various packages they may offer.

If you go to a large studio, be certain that the photographer that you talk to and see the work of is going to be the one that shows up at your wedding. Ask about their backup plan in case of illness.

Remember to have a clearly defined contract that specifies everything that you and your partner agree upon with them.

Here are a few important things to know before your employ any photographer:

+ Do they shoot in black and white, color, or both?

+ What types of cameras do they use?

+ Will they work with natural and flash lighting?

+ Will the shots be a mixture of posed and candid?

+ Can you ask for specific shots you want done?

+ How many rolls of film do they typically use for a wedding and reception?

+ Will the photographer stay the whole time for your ceremony and reception?

+ Are the negatives included in the price?

+ How long will it take before proofs are available?

+ After selecting from the proofs, how long does it take to receive the album/prints?

+ How exactly does the photographer charge for their services and the prints?

+ Are travel time and hourly rates included?

+ Do they offer any types of complete packages?

+ Do they develop their own pictures or send them out to a qualified lab?

Transportation

***

ow many cars do you need for the wedding and reception? It all depends upon the logistics of your wedding location and reception facility, your budget, and of course the style you're looking to create.

Customarily, the wedding couple has a chauffeured town car or limousine to go from the wedding to the reception, taking their time to have the horn honked around town announcing the nuptials. If the reception hall is just around the corner, or the wedding and reception take place at the same location, a horse-drawn carriage could be a substitute for something romantic to ride in. We've done that on numerous occasions where the church was right next door and within easy access.

Limousine service has become a tradition for most traditional couples. But you don't have to follow any unwritten rules. For instance, if you and your girlfriend have a Harley, you go for it, girls! (Just make sure if you're on the back and wearing a dress that you've taken precautions against getting wrapped up in that chain in a way you don't want to be!) And if you happen to have a friend who owns a '43 blue Packard convertible, consider asking them for the favor of helping you out with special wheels on your wedding day.

If you have decided to go the traditional route and hire a limousine, you could even consider getting more than one. One should be for the two of you and another one to drive the wedding party to the reception (that is, if you have a wedding party). One of the major advantages to the limo is that you can stretch out and relax, and even more importantly, you can stay wrinkle free! Another advantage is that it lets the two of you have some free breathing time spent alone together before heading off to the second act of the program. If you're lucky enough to have a tinted dividing window between you and the driver . . . then I leave the rest up to both of your imaginations!

Make your decision about the cars based upon how many people you will be transporting. You may want to consider using a service for pickups like your grandparents, elderly friends, or close family. Remember that chauffeured town cars are always less expensive than limousines. A limousine usually seats between four and six people, much more with a stretch.

Figure out what exactly you will need the cars for: taking people to or from the ceremony, taking them home, etc. If the driver has to wait for any length of time, it will cost you more. Many limo companies can charge you rates by the half or full day, too. This might be a great option that would work for you.

The majority of couples who use a limousine have the car pick them up and take them to the ceremony location, then after the ceremony drive the two of them around for a bit and head off to the reception. Later the car takes them home, on to their hotel, or takes the best man to pick up the married couple's decorated car. In between all of this, there could be pickups or dropoffs of other wedding guests, if time permits.

Be sure to ask the company if gratuities are included in the charge, as well as about their cancellation policy. Ask if you can add extras like a bottle of champagne, glasses, and ice in the back and what the charge will be. Make sure that you know exactly which car you'll be getting and the length of time that you'll be having it for.

Limousines, Rolls Royces, classic cars, and horse-drawn carriages all add to the romantic ambiance of your celebration. As you roll out the door and make your grand exit consider having a few fireworks, some special music playing in the background, or some other creative signal to add to that special parting moment.

Registering for Gifts

"He's like this wonderful shadow. I don't mean 'shadow' in a

negative way. I mean, he's always with me, even when he's

not. He's always right there beside me, even

if it's just in my heart"

FRED

sk any bride who's received three toasters if, if she had to do it all over again, she wouldn't at least consider registering for her wedding gifts! Registering is a chance for you as a couple to direct your guests to a place where they can find the gifts you really want. Why? Because you selected them yourself at one of your favorite places.

Gift registering not only insures that the two of you get those things you most need, but reassures your guests, who want to buy you those things, that they are choosing gifts you really need. In the long run, it saves both you and your guests time and energy, which makes everyone happy.

First, pick a store or two where you would actually shop for all the things you'll need for your new life together. Stores like Home Depot and Target have become popular, as well as Michael C. Fina (www.GayWeddingRegistery.com). Make sure the store encompasses your personal style.

Choose wisely as you register, and make sure that both you and your partner look around to decide what it is you'd really like. There are always the new dishes and china, glassware and crystal, but nowadays you can register for other things too, from luggage to honeymoon packages. The choices are endless.

The trick to letting your guests know where you are registered is through family, close friends, your parents, and your attendants. Have them spread the word for you, especially if you don't want those three toasters! Tell them where you are registered, and ask them to please tell anybody who asks what you would like where you are registered. Don't be bashful. Nobody wants to buy you a gift that you can't use. And it helps your friends and family be able to make choices that are in their price range, so you're doing them a service, too!

It's a good idea to register for gifts as soon as you announce the engagement. There are always people who'd like to get your gifts to you early and this way everything will be set up for them to do so.

Make sure you read the fine print on the registry program, and confirm that there is a wide range of gifts that appeal to you both. Carefully read the store's exchange and return policy for an understanding of what their terms are. Be sure also to find out if you can buy over the phone with a credit card or go on the computer to do your ordering. Does the company make it convenient for all of your friends and family to place orders? And what is the shipping time that it takes for delivery?

When you first register, also get the name of the salesperson who will set up your account, in case any problems arise later on, and keep checking on what selections have been purchased as time goes along, so that you can add new gifts to the registry if needed.

If you're concerned about how many gifts to put on your list, our answer is . . . the more the merrier! Don't hesitate to select a lot of different things that people can buy, because the more you choose, the more likely it is that your guests can find something they would really like to get you.

⊷

Thank-You Notes

Thank-you notes are a wonderful way for you to take a few moments to thank your guests in a formal manner. They are an integral and necessary part of the process, especially when they're written as a matter of sincere gratitude for someone's thoughtfulness. In their own unique way, they become the last piece of your wedding puzzle.

We recommend that you get your thank-yous out in the mail within a month or so (at the latest) after the wedding. Most couples will want to order their thank-you notes at the same time they order their invitations, but you don't have to have your thank-you notes continue the motif, if you don't want. Obviously it's important to make sure that the notes are personalized by you and your partner and don't look like they were written on a scrap of paper.

When writing your notes, you and your partner may want to split up the work, since usually these notes are written by hand. Be sure that you make a direct reference to the gifts you received in the note for each of your guests. If you received money, you don't need to mention the amount of money directly in the card, but refer to it as their "generous gift."

If you received a gift that you are not fond of or that you received more than one of, there is no need to comment on this in your thank-you note. Maybe you'll find a good home for it somewhere with a friend, who knows. There's no need to create any drama by mentioning the unwelcome gift to anyone else. Even if you are not thankful for the actual gift, you should be thankful for your guest's generosity, right?

In order to keep track of all of your gifts, keep a journal or chart as you open them up. This way, you can go down the line as you write your notes and check off each person or party until the notes are all completed.

Honeymoons

"I believe that our love is really about sharing, and believing
that the impossible can really happen. With him, the
impossible happens every day in my life."

NOAH

You and your partner need to sit down and start thinking about where you want to spend your honeymoon. This is not a chore—this should be one of the greatest and most fun parts of this whole adventure for you. Even if your budget is really tight, you can still consider having a honeymoon locally to get away for a couple days and be together alone. To my mind, honeymoons are simply a requirement.

Start your new life off right by giving yourselves quality time together right from the start. Have a cup of coffee (or tea) and begin by asking each other some questions to help define where it is you'd like to go and what you can afford. Remember: you can't afford *not* to have a getaway. You both deserve it after all the planning it took to make this whole gig a success.

Even if you have to put your honeymoon off for a while because of the cost of your wedding, consider not letting too much time pass before you take off somewhere together. If you need time to rebuild your bank account, take it, but remember that you both deserve the time you'll spend together on a getaway.

Start by planning the honeymoon well in advance, if you can. As a couple, the decision of where to go, the budget, and how long you'll be gone for should be made together. It's a time to celebrate your life together as a married couple and to learn more about each other during the romantic getaway. Make this a dream-of-a-lifetime vacation, even if your budget is tight and you can only travel locally. Put some thought into it, and enhance the romance you two already share.

Where do you want to go, a place full of sunshine or somewhere where you can ski and sit out in your private hot tub while it's snowing? What kind of setting do you dream of: beach, mountains, woods, ocean—where?

The most popular destinations for honeymoons are places with beautiful beaches. Hawaii has a reputation, along with the Caribbean, for being honeymoon heaven. Beaches by day and romantic candlelit dinners by night are the idea of ultimate bliss for many newlywed couples. Usually when the word "honeymoon" is mentioned, a vision of some tropical paradise is called to mind. There are other options, however, for those of you who want to do something different from the typical honeymoon trip.

You could consider a wooded setting in the Rocky Mountains for skiing by day and cuddling by firelight at night. Or pick a country you would love to visit. Maybe you've always wanted to go to Japan, but never had reason enough—a honeymoon is a great excuse to go anywhere. As long as the two of you can agree on a place to go that excites you, then your honeymoon is almost guaranteed to be a smash.

What are each of your top three choices of places to go for a honeymoon? Are they local or in another part of the world? How far are you willing to travel?

When trying to decide where you want to go, pick a destination that will give you both relaxation and rejuvenation, and allow you to have some great fun. When we are judging a honeymoon location we ask ourselves:

- How romantic is it?
- How affordable is it?
- Does it offer us at least some seclusion when we want it?
- Can we create an adventure here?

If you want to go to a foreign country, you could pick someplace as close as Mexico or someplace as far as Australia. If you have a budget, this will weigh heavily in where you decide to go. But what also weighs in your decision is how far you are willing to travel. If the thought of being on a plane for more than an hour or two has you squirming already, then maybe you want to stay closer to home. If you hate the idea of having to actually get from Point A to Point B but do not want to stay close to home either, why not turn your traveling time into the honeymoon itself traveling by train cross-country or taking a cruise (a wildly popular honeymoon idea). This way you can truthfully say it's the journey, not the destination, that counts.

Do you want to get married in the same place you will honeymoon?

You can consider taking the whole shindig, wedding and honeymoon, to a tropical location or other desirable locale. Most couples opt against this because it is such a costly endeavor; however, it is an option if you like the idea of getting married and then rolling out of bed the next morning already at your honeymoon. Make sure your family and friends know that you won't be accessible after the wedding. The one thing you don't want a honeymoon to be is a family affair!

Do you want to hire a travel agent or book the trip yourself?

These days, with the plethora of travel sites on the Internet, you can easily book your honeymoon directly. You can find great packages designed specifically for honeymoons on most of the travel sites on the web. Planning your own trip can be exciting because you have so many options and you'll get to pick and choose as you please. You can custom-design your trip over the Internet from start to finish. You can also purchase travel guides from a bookstore. You should start with booking your hotel. From there, you can even utilize the hotel for planning your meals and other activities.

But hiring a travel agent is not an outdated concept. Many couples still seek the aid of an experienced travel agent to guide them to paradise. The travel agent can handle everything from transportation to extracurricular activities in a snap. Travel agents are the experts at travel, and honeymoon travel makes up a large portion of their expertise. Not only can you get more information about the destination from your agent, you can ask for suggestions. You might even start with a travel agent if you are unsure of where to go. I guarantee you they will do all they can to help you find the right destination.

Travel agents can also help a great deal by making the planning process so much easier. In many large agencies there are special departments specifically set up to help with honeymoons. Also, many hotels and cruise ship lines offer packages that are all inclusive. Some even offer special off-season rates and other discounts. Be sure to ask.

Are you looking for a place that's hopping, with lots to do and see, or somewhere removed from it all where you can spend quiet quality time together?

Scuba diving, surfing lessons, a tour of the island . . . and that's just Monday. Do you want to fill your schedule with activities and always make sure you have something to do? If so, you'll have to do some research about local attractions and what's fun to do. The place you are going probably has a tourism website that can suggest fun and interesting things. Each place usually has a "must-do" list for tourists. You can even call a city's Chamber of Commerce, Visitor's Bureau, or

Tourist Board to request that a packet be sent out to you for more information about the area's hot spots.

Or, you can choose to have nothing at all planned and use your time to unwind after your big day. Having nothing to do can be great for a newlywed couple. Some of the most memorable honeymoons have been spent entirely in a hotel room. This leaves room for spontaneity and creativity as well. It's great to wake up in the morning and plan your day with a fresh perspective.

If you choose to have an active vacation (outside of the hotel room) be sure to have a tentative itinerary planned prior to your arrival. Some things will require pre-arrangement, so you want to be prepared.

Are you willing to splurge for this or will you have to budget and restrict your expenses?

Each of you should discuss with the other what your fantasies about a honeymoon are. Consider whether or not you'd rather get an all-inclusive package on a cruise ship or at a resort that can be custom-designed so your every need is looked after. Pretend that the sky's the limit, and then afterward bring it more in line with reality—see what you can do that comes close to your fantasy.

A Few Tips About Honeymoons

✦ Don't be shy about letting gay-friendly people and businesses know that you're on your honeymoon . . . you won't believe some of the perks you can get!

✦ Be very clear on what your needs will be, especially when you're dealing with travel agents, hotels, and airlines.

✦ Acquire as much information as you can beforehand about your destination and the things to do (or not do) in the area.

✦ Don't forget to make out an itinerary for your day's activities, or at least a list of things you might want to include such as a picnic, snorkeling, dinner at a particular restaurant, or even breakfast in bed.

- Check with friends and family who might have vacationed before in the area that you're going to. They might just have some great suggestions.

- Don't forget to bring along your camera and loads of film to make some memories. You might want to also consider bringing along a portable CD player and your favorite music to set the mood.

- Bring along any favorite bubble bath or oils for massage you might have. I'm sure you'll know what to do with them.

- Don't be afraid to try some new positions, in and out of bed. By the way, if you have any favorite "toys," here might be the time to loosen up and be a little daring and creative . . .

- Don't forget to try and catch the sunsets . . . there's something about seeing your partner in that golden glow that will stay with you for a lifetime! If you can make it to the ocean, it might just be a great place to go skinny dipping afterward.

- Be sure to ask your travel agent for any discounts available and book your reservations as early as possible to get the best rooms and to find the best deals. Try to use a frequent flyer credit card if you can and charge your wedding and honeymoon expenses to the card. Think of all the extra mileage you'll accumulate!

- We've been told by many honeymooners that they found it better to book in the top place, a little beyond their budget, and take one of their cheaper rooms, since they don't spend a lot of their time in the room except in bed. They get more added amenities that way, enjoy the beach or outdoors, and even get free room upgrades, on occasion, just because they're on their honeymoon. It's something to at least consider.

Things to Take

The following is a partial list of some of the forget-me-nots that will be indispensable to you on your honeymoon:

- Both of your passports (up to date)

- Luggage (obviously), but don't overpack—save some room to do some shopping
- Sunglasses and reading glasses or contacts
- Any necessary inoculation records
- Suntan lotion and moisturizers
- Any absolutely necessary wardrobe necessities

Some Practical Advice

1. Don't forget your camera and extra film.

2. Label your luggage.

3. If flying, put all of your necessities in your carry-on bag.

4. If you're going to a foreign country, you might want to take a calculator for currency exchange calculation and make sure you have all the necessary documentation you need for traveling to and from your destination.

5. Keep cash in a safe place, such as a hotel safe deposit box, when you are not in the room.

6. Try not to carry too much cash on your person when shopping on your honeymoon.

7. A consideration that you should both make is whether or not to get travel insurance that covers trip cancellations. If you unexpectedly have to cancel reservations the company reimburses you. It doesn't cost much for this coverage, but it is well worth having.

8. Make sure that you take time during your honeymoon planning to double-check all dates, times, confirmations, and plans. It may be a little extra work, but it's something that is absolutely critical to do so that your vacation runs smoothly and is totally stress free. You want this part of the wedding to be unforgettable in incredible ways, not a time when everything that could go wrong, did.

Your Honeymoon Budget

It's important, especially if you're on a tight budget, to know what your honeymoon will cost ahead of time. By taking the time to fill out our budget sheet beforehand, you'll decrease your stress before your trip and know more about the funds you have available for shopping and adding other activities or itineraries to your travel plans.

Project your expenses as best you can, guesstimating when you have to, but always try to guess at a higher cost if you don't know for certain. That way it will always cost less than you thought in the end.

A budget also helps you to know what the total bill will be, and gives you an idea of what it will take to pay it off if you're charging everything to your credit cards. Have a game plan ahead of time and you'll enjoy this part of the adventure even more!

If there is any way your budget can allow for your dream-of-a-lifetime getaway . . . this should be your chance to treat yourselves royally! Remember that your honeymoon budget should be carefully planned ahead of time. This pre-planning will make your trip all the more fantastic, so it's worth the effort. To get the ball rolling, here's a list of the top twenty vacation destinations for lesbians and gays.

Most-popular Destinations for Lesbians and Gays

Out & About magazine recently listed what they believe were the top 10 romantic destinations for gay couples around the world. It really didn't come as a surprise which locations around the world they found were most popular.

- Paris with the Eiffel Tower, the long strolls on the Champs Elysees, shopping, jazz and the allure of simply sitting at the many sidewalk cafes.
- The big island of Hawaii has an active gay community and there are many gay-run businesses. The islanders are very welcoming and the scenery is awesome—you'll love the beaches.
- Vermont and Massachusetts were included on the list because they

currently have the closest thing to marriage equality in the United States. Vermont offers serene mountain and forest scenery, beautiful any time of the year. Massachusetts has the ocean, Boston, and Provincetown with wonderful shopping, galleries, and restaurants.

✦ St. Bart's has spectacular beaches and dining. Personally, I would choose St. John over St. Bart's any day. Remember, that's just my preference. I find St. John more attractive because it is not as overbuilt as St. Bart's. The island was also included in "Top 10 beaches in the world" by *National Geographic*.

✦ Santa Fe, New Mexico, offers an incredible taste of the Southwest: mesas, charming adobes, limitless outdoor activity, and a hot art and culture scene. It's a popular spot for many lesbian couples.

✦ Prague, in the Czech Republic, offers historic architecture, accepting attitudes, and a fantastic night life.

✦ There's a lot to do in the fun city of Montreal: sightseeing, jazz, museums, and cuisine from all over the world.

✦ Cape Town, South Africa, is sophisticated and has incredibly fine beaches.

✦ Puerto Vallarta, Mexico, has old world atmosphere, friendly attitudes, and many gay businesses in the city's Old Town.

Some other fabulous destinations where you most likely can feel safe and comfortable:

✦ Britain	✦ Key West
✦ New York City	✦ Hawaii
✦ San Francisco	✦ Miami
✦ Palm Springs, CA	✦ Philly
✦ Chicago	✦ Las Vegas

✦ One of my personal favorite destinations is Italy. Whether you're on the beautiful island of Capri, the coast of Amalfi, walking the streets of Rome at night, enjoying opera at La Scala, or riding a gondola on the Grand Canal, Italy is at the top of my list of places to go for incredible food, scenery, friendly people, and of course, romance.

Honeymoon Expense Budget

Transportation Costs

For Airline Flights (if applicable) $

(Include the cost of your tickets, transportation to and from and parking at the airport, and miscellaneous expenses.)

For Driving (if applicable) $

(Include your gasoline, lodging on the road, meals, and tolls for the trip.)

Lodging $

(Include the package rate for your accommodations or multiply your daily room rate times the number of days you will be staying. Be sure to include the tax.)

Food Costs $

(Add up the number of breakfasts, lunches, and dinners you will be having. Guesstimate the cost for each of the categories and multiply it by the number of that category's meals you'll be having. Don't include wine or alcohol, as that is to be put in the next category. Be sure to add fifteen to twenty percent gratuities to your estimates.)

Wine and Alcohol $

(Include how many bottles of wine and drinks you will probably be having during your trip. Be sure to drop a hint that a gift certificate from your family for a nice bottle of wine at dinner would be a thoughtful gift!)

Snacks $

(Include this budget item for all those little tidbits you may be enjoying and multiply it by the number of days of your stay.)

Phone Call Expenditure $

(Include this because you will be making them. If you budget for it, you won't feel guilty about how long you stay on that phone!)

Activity Costs $

(If you're pre-arranging your activities, you should have a good idea of the costs involved. If not and you're a free spirit, finding things to do as you go along, think of the possibilities like horseback riding, scuba, golf, etc., and guesstimate the costs as best you can. Be sure to include in this any tickets you'll be buying for shows or entertainment. One more thing: yes, your gambling expenses have to be included in this category—they are part of what you'll be spending!)

Gratuities $

(Include in this everyone from the bellhop to the baggage carrier, and everyone in between.)

Tours	$

(Include here any sightseeing that may have additional charges, or tour costs not already covered.)

Other Expenses	$

(Anything not included in the previous categories that needs to be added in.)

Total Honeymoon Expenditure	$

Just a Few Honeymoon Enhancers and Ritual Suggestions

+ Breakfast in bed

+ Late-night swims

+ Bubble baths with candles

+ Massaging each other with oils and lotions

+ Meeting in the lounge for afternoon drinks

+ Getting someone to take your picture together

+ Leaving a love note or card on your partner's pillow with a rose or their favorite flower

+ Sunsets shared together

+ Arranging for chilled champagne to be delivered to the room

+ Creating little adventures in the daily itinerary

+ Spending a lot of time in bed—not just sleeping!

Remember that the honeymoon is the part when you both get to sit back, relax, and truly enjoy your first special times together as a married couple. It is the most anticipated part of the wedding for some couples because you finally get the chance to be together alone with the pressures of planning all behind you.

Your honeymoon should be an unforgettable time in your life. Take the time to plan it, then enjoy it and create those memories that will indeed last a lifetime.

For Uncertain Guests

"I looked around the room and all I saw was people who simply loved each other. I suddenly wondered what all the fuss had been about."

JANET, AGE 72, MARRIED WITH EIGHT GRANDCHILDREN,
AT HER FIRST GAY WEDDING

Okay, so you've been running the idea through your head that you may have a couple of guests who are wondering if they can really handle your gay wedding and don't know if they'll be attending or not. Hopefully, if this is the case, these guests know on some level that attending your ceremony would be the most wonderful gift that they could give to your and your future spouse.

If they really can't focus on the true meaning of this day and why the two of you want to have a ceremony, then it may be best that they don't attend. As hurtful as that may seem, it might be better to face facts (if you know for certain that they have issues) and deal with the hurt that comes up. However, I can assure you, having attended so many of these wonderful ceremonies, that it will be their loss if they don't attend!

It may be difficult to accept the fact that someone that you are close to or know very well has declined your invitation. Obviously you want these people to attend on some level. And it's also obvious that when you sent the invitation you didn't realize how much they were going to be so damn uptight about this stuff, and unreasonable . . . and . . . (Okay, I'll stop!)

To learn that some guests won't be attending will be a disappointment you might have to face. However, even though this probably won't cheer you up, statistically you can't expect that all of your invited guests will be able to attend. It's very rare at any wedding to get one hundred percent attendance.

The best thing one can hope for is that an uncertain guest will show good manners and find a small excuse to regretfully decline, even if there are major issues they are dealing with concerning who you are and who you are marrying. If they're unable to wish you well, then hopefully they will have the courtesy to show some good manners and say nothing at all.

Sometimes family and friends feel that if they do not express their honest opinions, they will be doing their loved ones a disservice. Because of this there are those who must openly express disapproval for their own ego gratification. This philosophy may help in other situations, but most likely it will only be hurtful to you both if one of your guests chooses to take such a route. Let's hope this doesn't happen. I am very sincere when I say that you absolutely don't need any of that crap, nor should you have to deal with it at this special time!

If they only knew how many hurdles both of you have had to jump over to get where you are, obstacles that straight couples never have to face. A gay couple who's decided to have a wedding ceremony in the company of friends and family has had to learn what true courage is when facing those hurdles, and learn how to overcome them.

You should not expect to be able to change their mind, even though you know deep down that attending your wedding would more than likely have helped them to broaden their perspectives and experience a positive change in how they view the world. Hopefully they will keep any of their negative personal opinions to themselves, which may very well be the best solution to this whole problem.

Whatever you might say in response to their decision not to attend has probably already been part of a discussion they've had with someone else. You're probably not going to be able to change their minds. In all likelihood they will need time to reflect, hopefully educate themselves, and perhaps one day be able to look at the issues from a new perspective.

If they are very close to one of you, just returning the response card may not suffice for them if they are being pulled in several directions by their feelings right now. If they can't get past those feelings, hopefully they'll realize that the best way for them to handle the situation is to gather the strength to tell you in person or over the phone that they can't attend the wedding for their own reasons. If they do this, you might think twice about taking it any further at this time and consider letting things be as they are. That decision, of course, is totally up to you.

If they are thoughtful enough to send you a graceful decline, please consider trying to let them know how much you care about them, and leave it at that for now. (That is, if you agree with this approach.) Obviously you already think a great deal of them, or you wouldn't have invited them to begin with. Give them time to sort out their feelings, if you can. Try not, if it's humanly possible, to slam the door on someone forever if you don't really have to.

The one great thing about all of this is that you know damn well they're going to hear from one source or another how inspirational your ceremony was . . . and what a hell of a damn good party they missed!

Which leads us to our next point . . .

Guest Etiquette

(for those who don't yet know . . .)

✦ Even if you can't attend the wedding, you should send a congrat-
ulatory note and a gift. If you do go to the wedding, arrange for
the gift to arrive at the couple's home so they don't have to deal
with transporting it from their wedding location.

✦ Only bring a date if your invitation says "and guest." This rule
applies unless you have a significant other, in which case it is
expected that you bring them. (Make sure the couple knows you
consider this person a significant other if their name's not on
that invitation!)

✦ Arrive on time—the ceremony will start without you otherwise.
Try to arrive at least fifteen minutes early, and allow for time in
case you get stuck in traffic.

✦ This day is about the couple, so everyone else should leave their
personal dramas at home. The couple getting married already has
enough drama going on in the new life they're trying to make
together.

✦ Don't take photographs during the ceremony, unless you don't
use a flash and don't get out of your seat. Respect the couple.
Exercise your good judgment.

✦ Don't drink too much and make an ass out of yourself. That's
downright bad manners no matter how you look at it.

✦ Send your RSVP back promptly, and if you have to cancel after
you've already accepted, do it as quickly as possible, because the
couple may end up paying for you if you don't let them know.

Remember: it takes a lot of courage for that couple to be standing
up there in front of everyone. Give them as much of your love and support as you possibly can!

A Connecticut Yankee Goes to Her First Gay Wedding

Yes, Virginia . . . there are gay weddings!

Virginia is a conservative eighty-three-year-old Connecticut Yankee. She is a staunch Republican who believes in hard work, family values, and giving back to her community. As a founding board member of an elder care center, she came up with a fundraising idea to be sold as an item in the center's annual silent auction: the board would coordinate a cocktail party for fifty guests, including providing service, hors d'oeuvres, and booze, to the highest bidder.

Of course, the board could have never imagined that a gay man whose grandmother was a patient at the facility would place the highest bid and want the cocktail party as part of his wedding reception! When the board president announced that the cocktail party was for a gay wedding, the board members said they would provide the drinks and hors d'oeuvres but couldn't possibly attend and provide the service due to other pressing commitments.

Virginia thought about it a moment and said, "What the heck—I'll do it." With that, one other board member half Virginia's age (which was seventy at the time) said she would do it, too. Virginia and her cohort conned two male friends to volunteer as bartenders and they were on their way to "working" a gay wedding for the first time.

I've known Virginia ten years and until I told her about this book I had never heard this story. Here's my interview with her:

When was your first gay wedding?

1990.

Did you have preconceived ideas of how it was going to be?

Oh, gosh yes! I thought everyone would be in drag!

Were your preconceived ideas accurate?

I couldn't even imagine what to expect. It turned out to be the best wedding I ever went to—and I've been to a lot of weddings, and had five weddings for my daughters! It was such a diverse crowd, all races and religions. Everyone was warm and happy. I was only to stay through cocktails; my "job" was done. I ended up staying through the whole reception. I didn't want to miss out on all the fun.

Did you have any fears about attending?

At first, I thought it might be scandalous somehow or a mockery of the institution of marriage. Then I thought of the people I've known through the years who were gay and truly wonderful people. I thought, "If they are in love they have every right to be together and have a ceremony." I must admit I did have a conversation about all this with my minister. I came to the understanding that if people are in love, then expressing commitment among family and friends is beautiful and admirable no matter what their sexual orientation.

Were your fears dispelled?

As soon as I arrived at the house to set up the cocktail reception, I noticed the lovely backyard setting, everything so tastefully planned and executed. Not knowing that I had arrived, one of the grooms had just gotten out of the shower and walked into the kitchen wrapped in a towel. We both were embarrassed! He came over and gave me a hug and thanked me for being part of his special day!

Do you find more similarities or differences when you compare this gay wedding to traditional weddings you have been to?

The whole ceremony and reception were very traditional, there really wasn't much difference. It was such a happy time and everyone was just so happy. Here's the one difference I remember. At the end of the evening, a few family members were getting ready to leave. Someone noticed that Aunt Sally had left her handbag behind. Sally's sister asked her fifteen-year-old son to grab the bag and bring it to his aunt's car. The son jokingly said, "Get real, Mom, I'm not walking out of here with a purse!" Everyone got such a kick out of that!

Did attending the wedding change your point of view on this subject in any way?

I realized how much it means to *everyone* to publicly acknowledge their love and commitment. A few days after my wedding, the grooms showed up at my door with a gift for me. It was a silver heart pendant. They said they chose that "because I have a lot of heart"! I wear it to this day.

Would you attend another gay wedding in the future?

Now that's a silly question. Of course!

———

The Regular Guy

Steve's wife and I have been very good friends for years. I'm gay and she's straight and married, so of course her husband and my partner get added into the mix of our friendship together.

My partner and I are the only gay people Steve has ever really associated with. He's what most people would call "just a regular guy." He'd rather hang out on the couch and watch TV than go to a wedding—straight or gay. He's far from a metrosexual—he gets his hair *cut,* not styled. He doesn't like wearing a suit, and the same color khakis and button-collar shirts have been his uniform since high school. He works with other "regular guys" in the construction equipment industry.

It was great to interview Steve. It made me feel even closer to him as a friend.

Did you have preconceived ideas of how your first gay wedding was going to be?

No, I knew the couple well and had good times with them at parties and at home many times. I figured, knowing them, that it would be a warm and elegant celebration with lots of laughter and fun.

Did your ideas turn out to be accurate?

It was even better than I expected. I found the ceremony more moving than a traditional ceremony because I had never witnessed a public expression of love by two men. It made me realize that gay and straight people strive to have the same things: love, commitment, security, and a partner for life.

Did you have any fears about attending?

None whatsoever. Although it was a little weird when I told the guys at work I was taking time off to attend a wedding and they asked who was getting married. When I told them two men, they thought I was kidding. After a bunch of lame jokes (all completely unoriginal), I think they realized it wasn't such a strange concept. I think they got convinced because I obviously had no problem with going to the ceremony. I've worked with these guys for over ten years; I was one of the guys. I felt pretty cool educating them on the realities of the gay community: that they want what we want.

Do you find more similarities or differences when you compare this gay wedding to the traditional weddings you have been to before?

Very similar. They were just two people celebrating their love with friends and family. Wait! There was one big difference. There were two grooms on top of the cake!

Did attending the wedding change your point of view on this subject in any way?

Attending the ceremony just reinforced how similar, yet individually unique, we all are. I'm lucky to have friends like those two "regular guys."

In Conclusion

Through our years at GayWeddings.com, we have seen hundreds of couples make this commitment to be together for a lifetime. We've seen the transition from a collective wariness (the community saying, "We can't do this, it's not even legal in most places!") to a collective jubilance ("We deserve this and are going to do it our way!").

Gay couples have realized that it can be a wonderful experience to share a public promise of a lifetime commitment to each other with their loved ones standing with them, among friends and family.

With laws changing and the gay civil rights movement progressing, the goals of making gay marriage legal will not fall by the wayside. The gay community realizes that our relationships should be recognized by the law, and the reasons given against our marriages are slowly dissolving.

In the meantime, gay and lesbian couples everywhere from California to New York are having public ceremonies in declaration of their commitment and love for each other. To partners in love, a ceremony, legal or not, can provide a means for understanding and a recognition (to ourselves and to others) that we are a truly a couple. It can help friends and family understand how committed gays and lesbians are, just like everyone else in a loving, married relationship. These weddings also allow us to show our partners the commitment we want to make to them.

When you stand on the altar saying your vows, something truly remarkable happens. Everyone around you will feel it, too, deep within their heart and soul. The question of it being right or wrong seems to disappear for a while, and you are simply standing there, two people in love sharing your happiness with the world. What a wonderful gift this has been to traditional couples throughout the centuries. What a wonderful gift it is to us that we are finally starting to take part in the recognition by society.

Hopefully this guide has provided you with the tools you need to make your wedding day as perfect as possible. There is so much to think about when planning your big event . . . you've discovered that now.

But in the end, all that matters is the love you have for one another. Keep that as your true focus and your special day will be unforgettable. Congratulations on taking this step into the new frontier. May you enjoy a long, happy, and prosperous life together. We sincerely congratulate each and every one of you.

K.C. DAVID
and the Staff @ GayWeddings.com

Resources

The organizations below are the frontrunners in the education of America on gay issues. We have provided contact information for each. If you don't feel you need to turn anywhere for information or help, please consider possibly getting involved with any one of these wonderful organizations.

1. HUMAN RIGHTS CAMPAIGN (HRC): America's largest gay and lesbian organization. The Human Rights Campaign "effectively lobbies Congress; mobilizes grassroots action in diverse communities; invests strategically to elect a fair-minded Congress; and increases public understanding through innovative education and communication strategies" (www.hrc.org).

    HUMAN RIGHTS CAMPAIGN
    1640 Rhode Island Avenue NW
    Washington, DC 20036-3278
    Front Desk: (202) 628-4160
    Toll-Free: (800) 777-4723
    Membership Toll-Free: (800) 727-4723
    For general HRC inquiries/comments, please contact
    hrc@hrc.org.
    For membership-specific inquiries/comments, please contact
    membership@hrc.org.
    www.HRC.org

2. LAMBDA: "LAMBDA is a non-profit gay/lesbian/bisexual/transgender agency dedicated to reducing homophobia, inequality, hate crimes, and discrimination by encouraging self-acceptance, cooperation, and non-violence" (www.lambda.org).

LAMBDA GLBT COMMUNITY SERVICES
216 South Ochoa St
El Paso, TX 79901 USA
(206) 350-4283
admin@lambda.org
www.lambda.org

3. GAY AND LESBIAN ALLIANCE AGAINST DEFAMATION (GLAAD):
    "The Gay and Lesbian Alliance Against Defamation (GLAAD) is dedi-
    cated to promoting and ensuring fair, accurate and inclusive represen-
    tation of people and events in the media as a means of eliminating
    homophobia and discrimination based on gender identity and sexual
    orientation" (www.glaad.org).

    GLAAD   GLAAD
    5455 Wilshire Blvd, #1500   248 West 35th Street, 8th Floor
    Los Angeles, CA 90036   New York, NY 10001
    phone: (323) 933-2240   phone: (212) 629-3322
    fax: (323) 933-2241   fax: (212) 629-3225
                                   www.glaad.org

4. PARENTS, FAMILIES AND FRIENDS OF LESBIANS AND GAYS
    (PFLAG): "PFLAG promotes the health and well-being of gay, lesbian,
    bisexual and transgendered persons, their families, and friends
    through: support, to cope with an adverse society; education, to
    enlighten an ill-informed public; and advocacy, to end discrimination
    and to secure equal civil rights. Parents, Families and Friends of
    Lesbians and Gays provides an opportunity for dialogue about sexual
    orientation and gender identity, and acts to create a society that is
    healthy and respectful of human diversity" (www.pflag.org).

    PFLAG
    1726 M Street, NW Suite 400
    Washington, DC 20036
    phone: (202) 467-8180
    fax: (202) 467-8194
    www.pflag.org

Recipes

Some of Harry's favorite
Hors D'oeuvres and Canapés

CRAB LUMP ENDIVE Endive leaf filled with lump crabmeat lightly dressed in green garlicless Aioli

BABY TOMATO Filled baby tomato with white bean lemon hummus

STUFFED SHRIMP Stuffed prawns, herbed goat cheese, aufin herb

SALMON MOUSSE Piped on dark bread with paprika

CURRIED CHICKEN With mango chutney on Belgian endive

COUNTRY PÂTÉ With chutney

SALMON MOUSSE Piped on endive with paprika

STUFFED MUSHROOMS With crab or sausage and cheese

Potato and Leek Soup

4 oz butter (1 stick)
5 cups chopped leeks
2 stalks celery, chopped
1 large onion, chopped
3–5 cups roughly chopped potatoes
2 quarts chicken stock
salt and freshly ground pepper or white pepper
$^1/_2$–1 cup of cream

Melt butter in soup pot; add leeks, celery, and onions. Stew slowly until golden and soft, about 10 minutes. Do not let mixture brown. Add potatoes and chicken stock. Cover and bring to a boil. Reduce heat and simmer until potatoes are cooked through—20 to 40 minutes (time depends on potatoes' age and how they are chopped). Mash vegetables or roughly puree in food processor. Heat cream and add to the soup along with salt and pepper to taste.

Serves 4–6

This soup minus cream is wonderful; it keeps well in the refrigerator and freezes beautifully. Reheat and add cream at serving time; the cream gives a nice richness to the soup.

If you are using canned chicken stock, a squeeze of lemon juice will give it a fresher taste. College Inn is recommended.

If you are short on leeks, add onion to make the 5 cups of leeks.

TO TURN THIS INTO VICHYSSOISE

Puree leek and potato soup (chilled) so it is blended. Use 2 full cups of cream (chilled). Serve with a sprinkling of chives on each portion.

Gazpacho (Chilled)

3 slices fresh white bread, preferably homemade, crusts removed

5 cloves garlic, peeled

3 tbsp. fresh lemon juice

10 ripe large tomatoes, seeded and cut into $^1/_4$-inch dice

2 bunches scallions, minced

3 cucumbers, peeled, seeded, and cut into $^1/_4$-inch dice

2 green peppers, seeded and diced

1 red pepper, seeded and diced

1 yellow pepper, seeded and diced

1 large can V-8 (46 oz)

3 tbsp. balsamic vinegar

5 tbsp. fruity olive oil

salt and freshly ground pepper to taste

croutons for garnish

Place bread, garlic, and lemon juice in a blender or food processor fitted with a steel blade and process to a smooth paste. Transfer to a large mixing bowl. Add all the veggies to the bread paste and toss to combine. Stir in the V-8, then the vinegar, oil, salt, and pepper. Puree half the soup in the food processor and combine with the remaining soup. Refrigerate until very cold. Serve with croutons as garnish.

Fig and Stilton Salad

FIG PREP

4 9-oz packages of figs
Clean figs by cutting off stem and slicing in half. Place in 2 qt. water with
4 cinnamon sticks
1 tbsp. nutmeg
$^1/_2$ cup honey

Bring to a boil and lower heat to simmer figs approximately 20–30 minutes until soft; do not overcook. Store figs in cooking liquid; cool before refrigeration.

Place greens on glass plate, arrange 4 each $^1/_2$ figs, 4 grape tomatoes, 2 tbsp. stilton cheese on top and dress with Warm Bacon Dressing (next page), $2^1/_2$–3 oz ladle and serve immediately.

Spinach Salad

(Warm Bacon Dressing on next page.)

4 oz. baby spinach
3 oz. Warm Bacon Dressing
4 spears Belgian endive
2 grape tomatoes cut in half

Sauté spinach 2–3 minutes with dressing in pan until semi-tender. Do not overcook. Arrange spears and tomatoes; put spinach in center of plate; top with flower garnish and serve.

Warm Bacon Dressing

4 lbs. bacon, julienne
8 large onions, diced
$^1/_2$ cup shallots, diced (8m)
$^1/_4$ cup garlic, diced (8m)
2 cups sugar
3 cups Dijon mustard
1 cup red wine vinegar
$^1/_2$ cup extra virgin olive oil
$1^1/_2$ cups parsley chopped

Sauté bacon, onion, shallots, and add garlic at end. Do not brown. In large bowl, mix all ingredients. Whisk in sugar. Mixture should blend together nicely. Tart, sweet finish. Semi-thick, chunky.

Warm Goat Cheese Salad

2–$2^1/_2$ oz. spring mesculun greens
4 grape tomatoes
2 1-oz. goat cheese balls rolled in fine-ground pistachio nuts
$1^1/_2$ oz. balsamic vinaigrette

Place greens on plate. Heat cheese 10–15 seconds in microwave depending on firmness; try to keep in ball form for proper presentation. Place atop greens. Place tomatoes around edge of plate; carrots can also be used for color. Drizzle dressing over cheese. Garnish and serve.

Warm Baked Brie

10 Granny Smith apples

4 10-oz. pkg. pitted dates

3 cups honey

4 cups ground pistachios

4.5 oz Brie individual serving

Dice peeled and cored apples; be sure to peel into lemon water to retain color of apples. Dice into cubes, cut dates into halves, then again into thirds—$1/2$-inch dice. Combine all ingredients into large bowl. Heat dates and honey in microwave to soften, then mix. Cool before refrigeration.

Spray sizzle plate and Brie, top with 4–5 oz. apple compote. Create round effect. Bake in 500-degree oven 10–12 minutes. Serve with strawberry or raspberry puree and Caras cheese biscuits.

Filet Au Poivre

$1/2$ cup julienne or diced prosciutto

$1/4$ cup small capers

4 tbsp. olive oil

1 tsp. salt and pepper mix

$1 1/2$ cup veal demi glaze

$1/2$ cup heavy cream

$1/4$ cup French brandy

Add oil to pan; heat, add prosciutto and capers. Sauté until hot. Add
brandy and flambé. Add veal stock and cream. Reduce to low heat.
Serve over filet.

METHOD

Fresh pepper (top and bottom of filet)

Bring 2 tbsp. olive oil to high heat. Smear meat on each side. Flambé
with 1–3 tsp. of brandy. Finish in oven at 375 degrees.

Braised Norwegian Salmon

6–8 oz. salmon filet
2 tbsp. fig glaze

Spread over fish, spray sizzle plate with oil, pour 3 oz. white wine.
Bake 15 minutes at 475 or until glaze is browned. Sauté 2 oz. baby
spinach in wasabi vinaigrette 1–2 minutes; use as base for salmon;
top with black sesame seeds.

FIG GLAZE

4 9-oz. packages figs, cleaned
2 10-oz. packages dates
4 cups white wine
3 cinnamon sticks
$1/2$ tsp. nutmeg

Bring ingredients to a boil, simmer 45 minutes, puree with wand, cool
then refrigerate.

Rolled Chicken Breast
with Prosciutto and Fontina Cheese

Chicken breasts, spinach, proscuito, fontina cheese, panko bread crumbs, white flour, eggs

Cut chicken breast in half and pound with mallet.

Lay out prosciutto on breast, spinach, and fontina.

Roll up and then coat with flour, egg, then bread crumbs (in that order).

Sauté chicken on all sides to seal.

Bake in oven with chicken stock and white wine until golden brown (8–12 minutes). Slice roulade and place on plate of 1 oz. chicken sauce.

CHICKEN SAUCE

4 oz. chicken base or sherry broth

4 oz. pork stock

1 tbsp. garlic

3 tbsp. roux

3 tbsp. shallots, minced

4 cups white wine

1 sprig fresh rosemary

1 bay leaf

1 tsp. white pepper

2 tbsp. olive oil

Sauté in oil shallots, garlic, pepper, bay leaf. Add stock and base.

Add wine. Reduce to taste.

Add roux to thicken sauce consistency.

Duck and Cherry Sauce

$1/2$ duck breast

Bring 3 tbsp. olive oil to high heat, flour both sides of breast. Sear duck, skin-side down first, in pan until golden brown. Flip, sear until breast puffs up. Finish with cream sherry (approximately $1/4$ cup)

Finish in oven 5–9 minutes depending on desired temperature.

Heat cherry sauce in white wine (4 tbsp.); reduce to thickness desired—not runny.

Heat mushroom compote with chicken stock until hot and dry. Place mushroom on base.

Place duck on top. Place sauce on top of breast.

CHERRY SAUCE

3 lbs. dried cherries
2 cups kirchraser cherry brandy
$1/2$ cup fine sugar

Add brandy to cherries. Bring to boil. Add sugar. Remove from heat after 10–15 minutes. Puree with wand. Mixture must have liquid to be pureed.

WILD MUSHROOM COMPOTE

1 large container dried wild forest mushrooms
6 oz. Minors demi-glaze base
2 large Spanish onions
3 cups cream sherry

Wash mushrooms well. Sauté onions in 3 tbsp. olive oil, add mushrooms, sherry, and base over medium heat. Stir generously. Do not break up. Mixture must stay formed. Reduce and add white wine until all liquid evaporates, leaving some sauce to bring mixture and keep moist.

Crab Cakes

3 cans pasteurized lump crabmeat

3 cans backfin

$^1/_2$ cup finely chopped red, green, and yellow peppers

$^1/_4$ cup shallots

$^1/_4$ cup parsley

$^1/_2$ cup mayo

3 tbsp. salt/white pepper

$^1/_4$ cup Dijon mustard

$^3/_4$ cup natural bread crumbs

Combine all ingredients.

Form 7-oz. cakes. Wrap individually.

CRAB CAKE COOLING METHODS

Place crab cake in Panko bread crumbs, pat bread crumbs into cake to create coating, shake off excess crumbs. Heat sauté pan with 1 tbsp. olive or sauté oil. Brown on both sides, but be careful because crumbs cook quickly.

Place in preheated oven 10 minutes. Sauté $1^1/_2$ oz. baby spinach in 1 oz. white wine; do not overcook, spinach should stand up a little. Place cake atop spinach, saving a little to place atop cake. Put sauce on side of cake.

CRAB CAKE SAUCE

1 cup diced tricolored peppers

$^1/_4$ cup shallots

2 tbsp. garlic

$^1/_4$ cup marinara or red sauce

$^1/_2$ cup clam broth
$^1/_4$ cup white wine
2 tsp. roux

Add all ingredients to pan, reduce until thick. Serve over crab cake.

Pistachio Encrusted Sea Bass

7-oz. sea bass filets
Coat with ground pistachio nuts

Place on oiled sizzle platter. Roll fish in oil to get nuts to stick to fish. Bake at 350 for 12–15 minutes. Heat lentils in sauté pan, add 2 oz. chicken stock. Heat until liquid reduces. Place on plate on center line. Place fish on lentils. Top with mint basil pesto.

MINT BASIL PESTO

Place the following ingredients in a blender:

1 sprig of mint
8 basil leaves
3 tbsp. grated fresh parmesan cheese
2 tbsp. pinole nuts
  dash of garlic

Blend while slowly adding olive oil to the mixture. Taste-test and continue to add oil until consistency of the pesto is smooth.

Potatoes Au Gratin

These are wonderful and makes certain that the potatoes arrive hot, not cold!

   12–16 yukon gold potatoes
   ¹/₂ cup butter
   2 large onions (yellow or white)
   ¹/₂ cup flour
   7 cups half-and-half
   1 tsp. salt
   1 tsp. white pepper
   5 cups shredded Gruyère
   2 bay leaves
   1 tsp. nutmeg
   6 tbsp. bread crumbs

In saucepan, melt butter; add flour; make roux.

Add half-and-half, bay leaf, white pepper, nutmeg and bring to boil/simmer.

Slice peeled potatoes on mandolin (¹/₈" thickness—not see-through).

Butter glass rectangular pan thoroughly.

Place potatoes in pan with lapping technique (potatoes, chopped onion, cheese, and sauce). Top with bread crumbs.

Bake in oven at 350 for 45 minutes with cover on, 45–60 minutes uncovered.

Setting time: 4–6 hours.

Harry's Cranberry Bread Pudding

(Just Because!)

1/2 large challah bread, about 8 oz.

2 cups half-and-half

2 cups heavy cream

pinch of salt

I vanilla bean, split lengthwise

6 eggs

I cup granulated sugar

1/2 cup orange juice

I cup dried cranberries

confectioners sugar

Heat oven to 350.

Cut crust off bread and cut into 1-inch cubes. You should have about 3 1/2 cups of cubes. Arrange on a baking sheet and toast in the oven until light golden brown about 10 minutes. Set aside to cool. Leave oven on.

In a saucepan, heat the half-and-half, cream, salt, and vanilla bean over medium heat, stirring occasionally to make sure mixture does not burn or stick to the bottom of the pan. When the cream mixture reaches a fast simmer (do not let it boil), turn off the heat. Set aside to infuse 10–15 minutes.

In a large mixing bowl, whisk the eggs and sugar together, whisking constantly, and gradually add the hot cream mixture. Strain into a large bowl to smooth the mixture and remove the vanilla bean. Add the bread cubes, toss well, and let soak until absorbed. Fold mixture occasionally to ensure even soaking.

In a small saucepan, bring the orange juice to a simmer. Add the cranberries and simmer until plumped and softened about 5 minutes.

Drain cranberries and set aside. Divide the cranberries among 6 ramekins, custard cups, or dessert cups (or use a deep baking dish), reserving enough to sprinkle on each pudding. Divide the soaked bread among the dishes, then pour any remaining custard over the bread. Dot with remaining cranberries.

Line a 2-inch deep (at least) roasting pan with paper towels. Arrange the puddings in the roasting pan, leaving room between them and making sure they are not touching the sides of the pan. Then fill the pan with very hot tap water until it comes halfway up the sides of the dishes. Immediately place the pan in the preheated oven. Bake until set and golden brown on top, about 30 minutes for individual puddings, 40–45 for one big pudding. Serve warm or chilled, dusted with confectioners sugar.

Makes 6 servings

This recipe easily doubles. When preparing it in advance, follow the recipe until the baking part but do not bake it. Chill the pudding in the refrigerator then bake the next day. You may need to add 5–10 minutes to the baking time in this case. Reheat by covering the pudding with plastic wrap and microwaving it for 45 seconds.

Acknowledgments

There are many people who have played a part in bringing this book to fruition through their inspiration and support. Not least of all are the many businesses, inns, wedding planners, and clergy that now make same-sex ceremonies possible all around this country.

These people are demonstrating that they support the gay and lesbian community by affirming that they are gay friendly. They recognize love is the same for everyone regardless of sexual orientation. I applaud them for helping same-sex couples to have the weddings of their dreams!

I would like to thank my editor, Katherine Carlson of St. Martin's Press, who made this book a reality, pushing me gently yet firmly when I needed that last push.

I want to thank my sister Dawn. You remain a constant inspiration to me. A special thank-you to my friends Carrie and Souby for their hours of hard work and determination making sure this task was accomplished.

I would like to also acknowledge the many clergy who perform these ceremonies. They know what the "Good Book" is really all about and realize the true meaning of unconditional love.

And, as corny as it may sound, I want to thank my mother, who when I told her I was gay about ten years ago had two responses. First, she asked me if she did anything wrong, like drop me on my head or something. (I assured her there was no choice in the matter of my sexual preference.)

Her second response will live with me in my heart forever. It was a response only a loving mother could give. She said, "I want you to look at me. Understand something . . . you're my son. I want you to know I love you forever . . . no matter what. Do you hear me?"

Doris, you see, there is hope for this world after all.

K.C. DAVID

Index